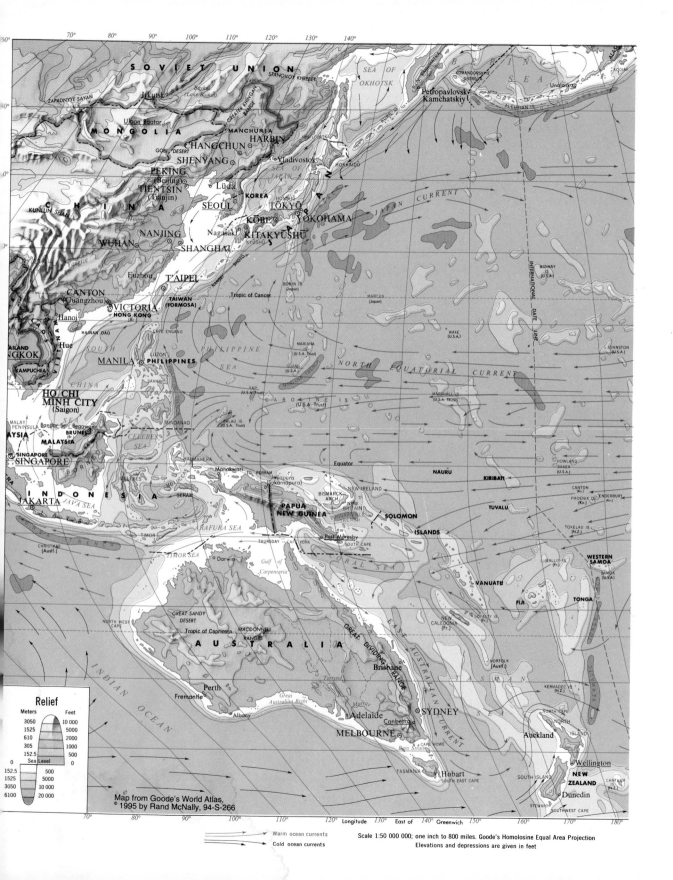

Scale 1:50 000 000; one inch to 800 miles. Goode's Homolosine Equal Area Projection
Elevations and depressions are given in feet

→ Warm ocean currents
→ Cold ocean currents

Relief

Meters	Feet
3050	10 000
1525	5000
610	2000
305	1000
152.5	500
Sea Level	0
0	
152.5	500
1525	5000
3050	10 000
6100	20 000

Map from Comprehensive World Atlas,
© 1995 by Rand McNally, 94-S-266

Longitude West of Greenwich

Enchantment of the World

SOLOMON ISLANDS

By Judith Diamond

Consultant for Solomon Islands: Michael W. Scott, M.A., Ph.D. candidate, Department of Anthropology, The University of Chicago

Consultant for Reading: Robert L. Hillerich, Ph.D., Professor Emeritus, Bowling Green State University; Consultant, Pinellas County Schools, Florida

CHILDRENS PRESS ®

CHICAGO

Palm fronds are laced together to be used as the roof of a thatched house.

Project Editor: Mary Reidy
Design: Margrit Fiddle
Photo Research: Feldman & Associates, Inc.

Library of Congress Cataloging-in-Publication Data

Diamond, Judith.
    Solomon Islands / by Judith Diamond.
        p.   cm.—(Enchantment of the world)
    Includes index.
    Summary: Discusses the geography, history, religion,
economy, people, and everyday life of the diverse peoples
of the Solomon Islands in the South Pacific Ocean.
    ISBN 0-516-02637-2
    1. Solomon Islands—Juvenile literature. [1. Solomon
Islands.] I. Title. II. Series.
DU850.D48   1995   95-2691
995.93—dc20   CIP
                                                  AC

Picture Acknowledgments
Animals Animals: © H. & J. Beste, 32 (right)
The Bettmann Archive: 47 (2 photos), 53

© **Cameramann International, Inc.:** 12, 22, 23, 34, 64, 65, 73, 81, 82, 87, 89, 101, 108 (left)
Ivy Images: 32 (left); © **Jonas/Shimlock,** 15 (left), 30, 31 (top right), 97
© **Wolfgang Kaehler:** Cover, Cover inset, 4, 5, 8 (3 photos), 9 (left), 16, 17, 19 (bottom), 21, 29 (top and bottom left), 54 (right), 55 (right), 58, 68, 71, 74 (2 photos), 76, 83, 90 (top), 96, 97 (inset), 109
North Wind Picture Archives: 36, 39
Photri: 54 (left), 55 (left)
Root Resources: © J. Downton, 9 (right), 94, 108 (right); © Lois Coren, 15 (right),
© **Bob and Ira Spring:** 19 (top), 20, 40, 46, 61, 84 (bottom), 90 (bottom left), 95
Tom Stack & Associates: © Mike Severns, 26 (top right)
Tony Stone Images: © Carl Roessler, 6; © Christopher Arnesen, 86; © David Austen, 90 (bottom right)
SuperStock International, Inc.: © David A. Northcott, 80 (right)
UPI/Bettmann: 57, 102
Valan: © Roy Luckow, 25; © Kennon Cook, 26 (left); © Dag Goering, 26 (bottom right), 28 (2 photos), 62, 67, 72, 79 (2 photos), 80 (left), 84 (top), 93, 103 (2 photos), 104, 105, 112-113; © Robert C. Simpson, 29 (bottom right)
Visuals Unlimited: © Hal Beral, 31 (top left, bottom left and right)
Len W. Meents: Maps on 14, 59, 63, 70, 78, 85, 91
Courtesy Flag Research Center, Winchester, Massachusetts 01890: Flag on back cover
Cover: Canoes tied up to palm trees on
                Rendova Island
Cover Inset: Young woman with flowers
                in her hair

Children of the Santa Cruz Islands

TABLE OF CONTENTS

A quiet, sunny beach by a turquoise lagoon

Chapter 1

SOLOMON ISLANDS' MANY WORLDS

The Solomon Islands chain, which stretches approximately 900 miles (1,448 kilometers) over the South Pacific Ocean, is home to some of the world's most diverse peoples. They live on raised coral reefs, atolls ringing lagoons of blue waters, and islands of steep mountains reaching almost to the shore. Some of these islands lie side by side; others are separated by sea journeys of days. Guadalcanal, the largest, is 2,500 square miles (6,475 square kilometers). Others are hardly more than jagged rocks breaking the sea's surface and can be walked in an hour. Tikopia, a small island near the eastern edge of the chain, supports a thousand people on each square mile. Some of the atolls in the western Solomons have fewer than ten people per square mile. On many of the 993 islands, there are no people at all.

Although English is the official language, the 300,000 people on these islands speak more than sixty other languages and many dialects. One village may not be able to understand the dialect of a neighboring village, although they are only a few miles apart. The language of everyday communication between separate language groups is Solomon Islands Pijin, an adapted form of

English with some words and most of its grammar taken from local languages. In Solomon Islands Pijin, the different language groups refer to themselves as *wantoks*, meaning people who speak "one talk," one language.

Religion, tradition, and ways of life are as different among the pockets of these mountains and the shores of these atolls as they are among the countries of Europe. The Solomon Islanders don't even all look alike. Skin tones range from the light golden brown of the Polynesians to the dark skins of some Melanesians, who have been referred to as the "blackest people in the world." Hair color and texture vary from deep reddish-blond to black and from curly and frizzy to long and straight.

Homes fit in with the geography and the style of the area. Generally, wood and bamboo houses thatched with leaves rest on the ground in the forested area called the *bush*, whereas they rise on stilts near the waters of the coast. There are places along the

Some houses are made from nature's provisions (left) and others are built using manufactured products (right).

edge of the sea, such as on the small island of Tikopia, where the houses are built close to earth and use the warm sand as a floor. In the towns, fiberboard houses with tin roofs provide shelter under palm trees. Around Honiara, the capital, located on the island of Guadalcanal, some modern hotels have been built in the hope of attracting foreign tourists.

Honiara, with thirty-five thousand residents, and other smaller towns in the islands are meeting places for Solomon Islanders who are visitors or permanent residents. Wantoks create their own neighborhoods, towns within town, but they are surrounded and influenced by the mixture of islanders and foreign peoples. They see and work beside wantok groups from other places in the Solomons. There are newspapers, magazines, and radios available here. Honiara also has high schools and colleges. Politicians, foreign businessmen, and tourists bring in the outside world. Even the food changes. The many types of sweet potatoes of the bush are expensive in the towns. People eat rice and tuna fish and drink colas or buy Popsicles and packages of crackers from small Chinese stores. Outside the town, a snack is sometimes as close as a piece of fruit hanging from a tree. In Honiara, unlike most other places of the world, people seldom buy food to snack on as they walk. There are no stands selling bags of nuts, ice cream, or meat on a stick. It is considered impolite to eat in front of others without being willing to share.

The diversity of the Solomons has been both an asset and a cause of conflict in the islands. When the islands were isolated from the world and each other, each Solomon Islander lived in his or her own world of tribe and tradition. Villagers were suspicious of neighbors. Speaking no common language and separated by forest and rock, it was easy for a misunderstanding to turn into a violent feud. Individual vengeance or open conflict between clans was common. In some areas cannibalism was practiced. Each small village group lived in alliance with a few nearby settlements. Most people rarely left their own territory. On the coast the sea gave people greater freedom to explore, but they too were limited by taboos and hostilities.

Within each language group customs and traditions spread a web of security and protection. To be born into such a group was to know exactly who you were and the role you would play in your society. No one was alone. Each individual or small cluster of villages was like a large, extended family protecting and caring for all its members. The smallest child felt a part of the whole, sharing in the history, the stories, and the land of his or her ancestors. Even today children form part of large extended families and clans, not just their nuclear families. They may be raised or adopted by distant relatives or even other people in the village or adjacent villages. In some areas where brides are bought, the person or group giving the largest contribution to the bride price will have the option of naming the first child and also may choose to adopt him or her. It is common for town dwellers to send their children back to live in the village so they can learn and remember the old ways.

The tremendous diversity of the Solomons has helped keep them from being easily conquered. "Big men" chosen in each village had power and respect, but major decisions were made by all the elders together. No one chief or group of chiefs determined the actions of their people. The Europeans threatened the Solomon Islanders with powerful ships and weapons and bribed them with axes, tobacco, cloth, and money. They brought their religions and their languages to the Solomons, but they could never totally control the islands. There were constant small uprisings and attacks on foreign missionaries and policemen. The Europeans eventually owned plantations, established provincial rulers, and published laws; but the villages maintained their own worlds of custom and tradition.

Now the Solomons are an independent nation with elected leaders. Diversity still pulls the islands in conflicting directions. The many different groups and cultures often focus on separate rather than similar needs. It is the goal of the leaders of this new country to use pride in independence to build national unity. They hope to join these diverse cultures without destroying their distinctiveness. The coast, the forest, the town, the village, those educated and those not, distinct races and distinct traditions give the Solomons their character and their challenge.

The islands are the tops of submerged mountain ranges.

Chapter 2

OCEAN ATOLLS
AND MOUNTAINS

The Solomon Islands lie on the southwestern edge of the Pacific Ocean 3,000 miles (4,828 kilometers) from the southern tip of China, 1,000 miles (1,609 kilometers) from Australia, and more than 6,000 miles (9,656 kilometers) from North America. They are in an area of the Pacific that the French explorer Dumont d'Urville in 1831 named *Melanesia,* the "Black Islands," as he remembered the sight of their dark, jagged forms rising from the green ocean.

The sea floor near the Solomons is made up of deep, folded trenches and crisscrossed mountain ranges. The islands are stepping stones out from Indonesia and Papua New Guinea, shaped from the summits of these submerged mountain ridges.

The islands scatter in a double chain. Choiseul, Santa Isabel, and Malaita follow one another on the South Pacific Ocean side. Shortland, Vella Lavella, New Georgia, Russell, and Guadalcanal are on the Coral or Solomon Sea side. The chains meet at Makira (San Cristobal) Island. East of the chains are the Santa Cruz Islands. Distant from the main group of the Solomons are the islands of Bellona and Rennell 100 miles (161 kilometers) to the south; tiny Sikaiana and Luangiua (Ontong Java) 200 miles (322

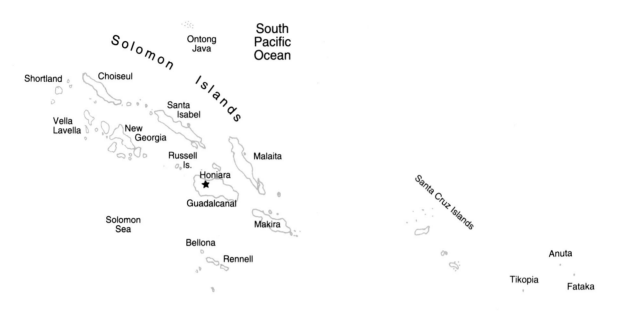

*Some islands mentioned in the text, when drawn to scale,
are too small to include on these maps.*

kilometers) to the northeast and north; and Anuta, Fataka, Pileni,
Taumako, and Tikopia 500 miles (805 kilometers) east of the
central cluster of the Solomons. These are the Polynesian outliers.
They are called outliers because, although their population is
Polynesian, they are separated by miles of ocean from the other
Polynesian islands. Hundreds of smaller islands, like the broken
pieces of a necklace, lie along the 900-mile (1,448-kilometer) line
stretching southeast from Papua New Guinea.

The six major islands are Choiseul, Guadalcanal, Malaita, New
Georgia, Makira, and Santa Isabel. Choiseul is the smallest, at 980
square miles (2,538 square kilometers), and Guadalcanal is the
largest. The islands are divided into nine provinces: Bellona,
Central, Guadalcanal, Isabel, Makira, Malaita, Rennell, Western,
and Choiseul. The capital territory of Honiara is another, separate
area.

Guadalcanal and the similar high central islands were formed

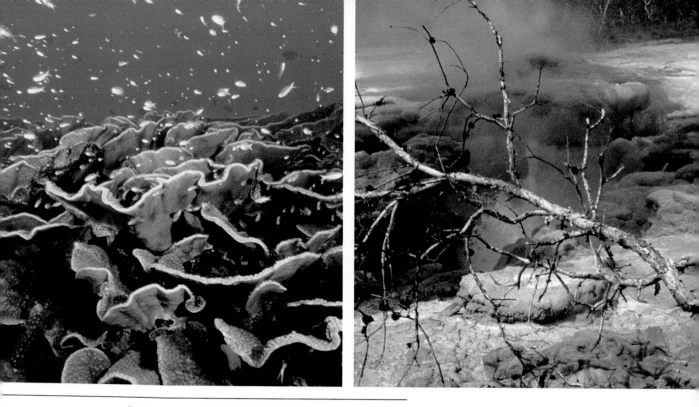

Lettuce coral formations (left) and hot springs (right)

from ancient volcanoes and lava flows. Ontong Java and the other fringe islands are coral. Coral is created by microscopic sea creatures that attach themselves to a rocky base. As they multiply, they secrete lime which, over centuries, forms spots of land. These islands are either thrust up from the sea by earthquakes or left as a ring when a mountain collapses.

A 300-mile (483-kilometer) belt of volcanoes called the Pacific "Ring of Fire" snakes through the Solomon Islands and Papua New Guinea. Submerged volcanoes erupting in boiling seas and island volcanoes have reshaped the land around them. The most recent major eruption was in 1971, when Tinakula near Santa Cruz ejected fire and ash and drove people from their homes. In addition to the volcanoes, the thermal activity on some of the islands creates sulfurous fumes, hot bubbling mud, and springs of warm water. Earthquakes are more common than volcanic eruptions. Although these seizures of the earth usually are not

A typical island scene of a sandy beach fringed by coconut palms

serious, there is always the potential for destruction or creation of new islands.

A typical island is surrounded by sandy beaches and fringed with clumps of coconut palms. It is intersected by rivers formed from mountain waterfalls emptying into swamps by the sea. Barriers of coral reefs offshore guard the island from rough seas and provide safe harbors.

MALAITA

Malaita, while the most populous, is one of the most rugged islands. On the east side, the mountains rise sharply from cliffs scarred by waves. Except for a few natural harbors suddenly breaking the coast, the ocean does continual battle with the shore. The west coast is protected by small groups of swampy islands covered with ivory nut trees and mangroves, whose roots rise

Men of Malaita perform a traditional dance.

bizarrely out of the soil. The center of Malaita is mountainous. There is little level land.

The daily rains keep the red clay sticky around the occasional *sinkholes*, hollows where water collects, where submerged streams make the ground treacherous. In the highlands there are vast areas of dense rain forest that let in little sun and allow few flowers to grow. But in the open, the colors are brilliant: green forest, turquoise lagoons, billows of white clouds and, in the distance, the rich blue of the Pacific.

One of the most interesting types of settlement in the Solomons are the man-made islands. Two of the most famous island areas are the Lau Lagoon on the northeast coast and Langalanga Lagoons on the west coast of Malaita. Here, to escape the equally dangerous enemies of hostile tribes and disease-carrying mosquitoes, the people of the seaside have built their own islands. Several thousand settlers live on these artificial platforms constructed of sand and chunks of coral in the shallow places of each lagoon. The islands, begun by one or two young married couples, grew as the families living on them grew. To build an island, first a spot is marked in the lagoon with a tall pole. Then stones are gathered and rafted to the site. On completion, the mass of rock rises 7 to 12 feet (2 to 3.6 meters) above the surface of the water. The whole process can take six months to a year. The lagoons are now quite crowded. People live closer together here than anywhere else in the Solomons, except perhaps in Honiara.

GUADALCANAL

Guadalcanal lies across from Malaita. It is the second most-populous island with fifty thousand people, excluding the population of Honiara, compared with the eighty thousand living on Malaita. Santa Isabel is third with a population of only fifteen thousand.

The present capital, Honiara, is on Guadalcanal. A road follows the north coast of Guadalcanal. On one side is the sand and sea, and on the other, wooded hills. Factories east of Honiara, shops, schools, and homes follow the road into the capital. Honiara stands on an old ammunition dump near Henderson Airfield, used by the American military during World War II. It was chosen as the capital primarily because of the wartime destruction of the former capital, Tulagi (in the Florida Islands), and the improvements that had been made by the Americans. Honiara has

Above: An aerial view of Guadalcanal, the biggest island
Below: A street in Honiara, the current capital city

The port at Honiara is the largest in the Solomon Islands.

one of the two ports in the Solomons that can service oceangoing ships. Gizo, near the large island of Vella Lavella, has the other port. There is a museum in Honiara and a botanical garden, churches, a hospital, a radio station, and banks. The national Solomon Airlines Company, as well as other foreign airlines, flies out of an airport near Honiara. The first large shopping complex, the NPF Plaza, was finished in 1986. Three hotels, run in partnership with foreign investors and managers, are in or near the town.

Honiara is the seat of the Solomon Islands government. It is also the home of the British High Commission and the governor-general who represents the British monarch on the islands. There are spacious government buildings, both from colonial days and newly built, with beautifully landscaped grounds and air-conditioned interiors. Honiara also boasts a nine-hole golf course

A view of Gizo

and the Guadalcanal Club, with a swimming pool and tennis courts. The main street, Mendaña Avenue, is lined with carefully tended lawns and red-flowering poinciana trees.

Honiara would be small if a city anywhere else, but it is the center of business, diplomacy, and trade in the Solomons. It attracts more people than it can employ. It has doubled in size since becoming the capital and has all the problems that rapid growth can bring.

OTHER TOWNS AND SETTLEMENTS

The growing westernization of Honaira and the few other provincial centers—the old capital of Tulagi, Auki in Malaita, Gizo in the Western District, and Kirakira in Makira—is in sharp contrast to the villages in the rest of the Solomons.

A village in a cleared area of the rain forest on Guadalcanal

High in the mountain regions are the smallest settlements, often no more than one or two houses in a clearing. Edging the islands are settlements that range in size from coastal hamlets sheltering five or six families up to bigger villages of just under a thousand.

CORAL ATOLLS

Ontong Java is a group of low coral atolls cut away from the coral reefs by the unceasing assault of ocean waves. The atolls lay just above the sea. Most of the land is too salty for growing crops. Freshwater from underground streams is only available on the largest islands. People on islands without freshwater cook with seawater and collect rain for drinking.

About 100 miles (161 kilometers) south of Guadalcanal are two other raised coral atolls, Bellona and Rennell. Rennell is one of the largest existing high coral islands. It is 49 miles (79 kilometers)

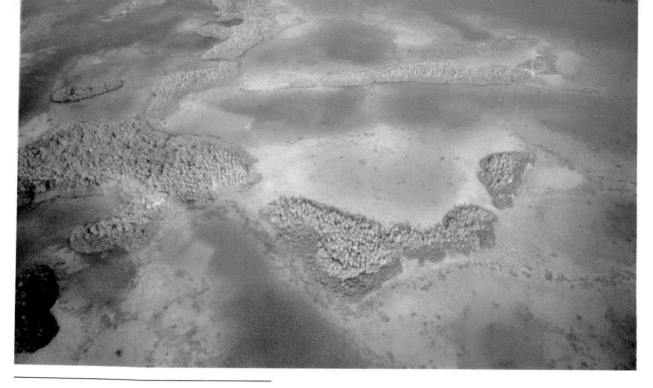

A bird's-eye view of coral atolls

long and 8 miles (13 kilometers) across. In a tale told by Solomon Islanders, the gods plucked Rennell from the sea upside down, rested the smooth side on the ocean floor, and left the rough jagged surface to rise above the waves. At Rennell's eastern edge is Lake Tegano, the largest lake in the South Pacific. Rennell and Bellona are picturesque tropical islands with rain forests, flowers, sand, and sea.

Anuta, Fataka, and Tikopia far to the east are just dots on the map isolated by miles of ocean from any other land. They are the last tips of the undersea volcanoes that form much of the Solomons. Tikopia has a lake in its center, the crater of a sunken volcano. Its beaches and steep hills are home to only two thousand people. But because the small island has an area of less than two square miles (five square kilometers), the population density is high. A thousand Tikopians have migrated elsewhere. Overpopulation is a developing problem on many of the smaller islands.

CLIMATE

These isolated islands that are separated from the rest of the Solomons suffer the most from the seasonally violent weather that batters this area. The cyclone season lasts from December to April. Although only two or three storms develop into actual cyclones, heavy rains are frequent. There will be a long period of calm weather, and then a storm will sweep in from the west, gathering in intensity, stripping the leaves from the branches, and uprooting the trees. Winds blast through the islands at 115 miles (185 kilometers) an hour. Salt spray stings the eyes and burns vegetation. The ferocity of these storms can destroy the year's gardens and rip the palm and bamboo houses from the ground.

There is a tremendous variation in rainfall amounts throughout the Solomons. Even on one island, the windward side can be quite wet and the other side much drier. The eastern section is the stormiest. Honiara in Guadalcanal gets 85 inches (216 centimeters) of rain a year, compared with 200 inches (508 centimeters) in Vanikolo, one of the southerly Santa Cruz Islands.

From May through October, the weather pattern reverses, blowing in from the east instead of the west. A sunny, quiet, gentle, windy day may be interrupted by a brief squall of rain in the afternoon. During this season, the winds are much steadier and calmer and the weather is more predictable.

Seasons are separated by rain and activities, not temperature, as the temperatures seldom vary. There is "the nut gathering season" or "the bonito fishing time." It is rarely hotter than 80 degrees Fahrenheit (26.6 degrees Celsius) or cooler than 70 degrees Fahrenheit (21.1 degrees Celsius). Comfort depends on the elevation and natural exposure to the wind as well as rainfall.

Frangipani blossoms

Chapter 3

ON WINGS, WATER, AND AIR

Everywhere on the Solomons there are fruits. Man and animals eat nuts from the areca palm, the cannarium almond, and most important, the coconut. There are wild figs, bananas, papayas, and Malay apples. In the low hills, great stretches of coarse alang-alang grass and ferns provide protection and cover for small mammals and birds.

On some islands, trees cover 90 percent of the land. The kaviko tree, the coral tree, and the poincianas bloom in reds from crimson to vermilion. Orchids are everywhere. There are 230 varieties in the Solomons—some that bloom nowhere else. One type has white flowers three inches (eight centimeters) across. Another changes color as it changes islands. It is yellow and brown on Guadalcanal, white on Malaita and Makira, and light purple on the Nggelas. Frangipani fills the air with perfume. Bougainvillea vines crown houses and trees with red and purple. Other flowering plants include begonias and hibiscus. Even the rivers bloom with water lilies.

Above: The trunks of banyan trees are gigantic. Monitor lizards (top right) sometimes grow to 5 feet (1.5 meters) in length and bougainvillea (right) thrive in the Solomons.

With food, water, security, and space, some animals and plants grow to great sizes. In the rain forest a tree might stretch 150 feet (46 meters) toward the sun. The main trunk of a banyan can be 30 feet (9 meters) in circumference. Its secondary trunks, formed from aerial roots that drape from its branches, may be as large as 4 to 6 feet (1.2 to 1.8 meters) around.

Eight-inch (20-centimeter) black spiders with yellow spots scurry near spiny, red ones that are not much smaller. There are 9-foot (2.7-meter) pythons and Rana guppyi frogs that weigh 2.5 pounds (1.1 kilograms). Also on the islands, though rarer now than in earlier days, are monitor lizards that can reach 5 feet (1.5 meters) in length and the largest freshwater crocodiles in the world.

BUTTERFLIES AND BIRDS

Hundreds of butterflies, from tiny, brightly colored specks to one with a wingspan of eight to eleven inches (twenty to twenty-eight centimeters), flicker in and out among the trees. Each type of butterfly seems to be trying to outdo the other in color combination and design. Some, like the eight-inch (twenty-centimeter) blue birdwind butterfly, which is a velvety black fringed with purple, breed only in the Solomons.

The forests are filled with birds. Tiny scarlet honeyeaters and yellow flowerpeckers join butterflies in sucking the nectar from the flowers. There are parrots in a rainbow of colors and sizes, including the world's smallest, the pygmy parrot. Many of the birds in the Solomons are familiar: hawks, eagles, storks, owls, and herons. But there are some that are adapted to only the Solomons and areas nearby. Still others have made the islands just one stop on journeys of hundreds of miles aloft ocean winds.

Among the more unusual birds are the crested swifts, who fashion tiny cups of bark and feathers into nests, each egg fitting inside exactly like a nut in a shell. The female swift glues her nest to a twig with spit and then sits astride it, her belly folded over the branch.

Another bird, the megapode, creates a vast mound of leaves and soil that may be 5 feet (1.5 meters) high and 20 feet (6 meters) in diameter. Eggs are buried in the mound and kept warm by fermenting leaves. Unlike the swifts, the megapodes, with their large feet and clumsy bodies, are poor fliers. They prefer running along the ground eating seeds, crabs, and fruit

Megapode birds (left) build mounds of leaves and soil (right) where they bury their eggs.

fallen from the trees. They make their short, noisy flights only when forced.

The frogmouth bird sits on a platform of sticks or feathers that it has disguised with bits of spider web or leaves. Then it opens its flat, triangular bill to reveal a large brilliantly colored inner mouth. Insects attracted by the color drop in for dinner.

The most famous bird of the Solomons is the frigate bird. It is the emblem of the islands and was sacred to some cultures. Its design is carved onto jewelry and printed on stamps. The frigate bird's body weighs 3 to 4 pounds (1.4 to 1.8 kilograms). It has a crest, a black head and back, and a white underbelly. The male has a red pouch on its throat, which it swells to attract the female. It nests in a haphazard pile of sticks on the ground. Without a good wind, the frigate bird has difficulty becoming airborne. Once in the air, however, it can hover for hours, its wings spanning 6 feet (1.8 meters) or more. It is considered the most agile flier of all seafowl, swooping down to steal food from other birds or plucking flying fish from the ocean.

Above: A female (left) and male frigate bird sit on their nest. To attract the female, the male frigate bird inflates his throat pouch (below left). The frogmouth bird (below right) has a bright inner mouth with which it lures insects.

An underwater coral reef

INSECTS, REPTILES, AND FISH

Less pleasant, crawling on the ground and flying in the air, are the myriad insects and small reptiles. There are sand flies, centipedes, scorpions, bees, houseflies, and cockroaches. Twenty distinct species of mosquitoes thrive in the warm, wet weather. In the past ten years ants, hitchhiking on ships, have arrived to become a real nuisance in some areas. Geckos and skinks (small lizards) creep across the ceilings and scurry along the corners of rooms. A tree dweller, the prehensile-tailed skink is the only lizard in the world that can hang by its tail.

The seas are rich in fish. Bonito (a type of tuna) and their relative, tunny, along with mackerel and porpoise, are caught commercially. Shellfish and *bêche-de-mer* (sea cucumbers) also are netted and sold for food. There are barracuda, sharks, and long-

Many tropical fish are brilliantly colored. Clockwise from above left are: a coral rock cod, a silvertip shark, a clown triggerfish, and a gaimard wrasse.

nosed garfish. The finback, the sperm, and the sulfur-belly whales swim in the deeper seas away from the shore. Weaving through the coral reefs, tropical fish make a garden of colors. Among the mangrove swamps, a strange fish called a goby climbs on the trees, grasping the branches with its pectoral fins. Other fish have eyes that have migrated to the edges of their bodies or translucent scales and visible skeletons. The variety and number are enormous.

MAMMALS

The smallest category of animals living on the Solomons is the mammals. There are several kinds of rats who nest both on the ground and in the trees. There are also bats, especially the fruit-eating bats known as flying foxes. Smaller bats help keep the

A bat (left), called a flying fox, and a cuscus (right)

mosquito population down. Both opossums and cuscuses are common marsupials who carry their young in a pouch on their belly. Cuscuses are monkeylike animals, about the size of a cat, who live in trees. They are silvery gray or brown with a long, strong prehensile tail and large, protruding eyes. Cats and dogs live in the villages and sometimes escape to become wild in the woods. Cattle have been brought to the Solomons since the early years of the twentieth century. They are still imported occasionally. Eleven thousand were shipped to the Solomons in 1970 to graze between the coconut trees on the plantations. Village pigs are raised for feasts, and long-snouted, ridge-backed wild pigs root for grub in the forests. Otherwise, mammals are few. The distance from the mainland is too great for larger mammals to swim. So mammals on the Solomons either had to evolve naturally or were brought in boats.

Chapter 4

THE ARRIVAL OF EXPLORERS: ÁLVARO DE MENDAÑA

The Solomons were unknown to the Western world before the sixteenth century. They were just small islands in the Pacific, far from the coast-hugging routes of the trade ships. But the ships became stronger and the knowledge and ambition of the pilots greater. Countries hungry for empires sent out explorers to find new lands. In some of these lands, the Western explorers found kings, civilizations, and what they really wanted—gold.

The Spanish had conquered Peru and looted the treasures of the rich Inca nation. They were restless. Rumors of new islands of wealth and a magical Inca king somewhere in the Pacific reached the ears of Peru's Spanish governor, Lope García de Castro. Perhaps de Castro believed the tales. Perhaps he was persuaded by his adventurous nephew, Álvaro de Mendaña. Whatever the reason, he encouraged the twenty-five year old to form an expedition to search for the islands and the gold on them.

On Wednesday, November 19, 1567, Mendaña left Callao, the port of Lima, Peru, with 150 men, 70 soldiers, and 4 friars from the order of St. Francis. The explorers filled two ships, *Los Reyes* and *Todos Santos*.

These decorated Islanders paddle a large canoe that is seldom seen today, but was common when Mendaña visited the Solomons.

Fifty-eight days passed on the open seas. Food and water ran low. No land was in sight. Talk of mutiny began. Then the ships passed the Ellice Islands and, after seventeen days, sighted Ontong Java. Despite sharp coral reefs and a cyclone, they made harbor six days later on February 7, 1568. The crew bowed their heads in prayer and christened the island Santa Isabel in honor of the patron saint on whose day they had sailed from Callao.

These strange Western ships with their high wooden sides and billowing sails seemed as if they had floated down from another world. The long, decorated canoes of the Solomon Islands pulled out from the shore to take a closer look.

Both the men in the ships and the ones in the canoes were young, probably still teenagers. Each side was excited, curious, and a little afraid. To the Solomon Islanders, the Spaniards were magical. To the Spaniards, the Solomon Islanders represented excitement, adventure, and the possible realization of their dream of gold.

In the beginning, the two sides stayed far from each other. Then the Spaniards made signs of the cross. They tossed their hats in the water to tempt the islanders to come closer. Finally a sailor jumped overboard and swam to a canoe.

By the afternoon, the two sets of strangers were facing each other on the Spanish deck. Mendaña offered a small feast of ship's provisions. The Solomon Islanders enjoyed the meat and preserves, but made faces at the wine and refused the crackers. Then the guests explored. They grabbed whatever was loose and inviting and sent it flying down to the more cautious who were still in the canoes.

Later that day, Bilebanara, one of the headmen of the island, visited the ship. He greeted the captain as one chief to another. His face was painted and he had a headdress of colored feathers. Armlets of bone decorated his wrists and a small shield hung around his neck. He promised to supply food and aid to the Spaniards. They promised to help him attack his enemies. That night both sides must have had glorious visions of their opportunities to profit from each other.

At first they kept their promises. The Spaniards navigated the island waterways and, with the islanders' help, explored and named the islands. The largest was called Guadalcanal after Pedro de Ortega's village in Spain. The next in size, Malaita, was named accidentally when a Spaniard asked what it was called. "*Mala eta*," or "There is Mala," answered his guide.

The optimistic beginning, however, did not last. Bilebanara could not feed so many men. The Spaniards could not empty their ships of food or they would not survive the trip home. The Spaniards consulted their friars. "Hunt or barter," the friars counseled, "but if that fails, take the food you need by force."

The Spaniards used arquebuses, awkward guns that were fired from the shoulder or, more often, from a support.

Each side first negotiated and then threatened. The Solomon Islanders circled the ships, shaking their war clubs and letting loose volleys of arrows. The Spanish soldiers camped on land and took turns sleeping and guarding the night fires. They shot their clumsy guns, called *arquebuses,* into the darkness to frighten away unseen presences. In the end, the Spaniards were stronger. The need for food, the desire to explore, and fear closed their minds to patience. They captured canoes and took the islanders hostage for food or forcibly held them as interpreters and guides. The hostilities climaxed with an attack by the islanders on a group of explorers collecting fresh water. Nine seamen were murdered.

In reprisal, the Spaniards swept the villages, looting and then burning them to the ground. Mendaña and his men did not leave the Solomons until August 11, six months after they had arrived and two and a half months after the incident. But there was no gold found, only suffering and disappointment on both sides.

The only things Mendaña and his sailors brought back to Peru were captives and stories. The captives, a man, woman, and child, died either on the way back or shortly after their arrival. The stories grew with the telling. Nobody knows who first connected the islands with the biblical King Solomon and his mines of gold. The first recorded mention was in the journal of the ship's pilot, Pedro Sarmiento de Gamboa. The journal was titled: *The Western Islands in the Southern Ocean, commonly called the Isles of Solomon.* The idea of a "King Solomon" and mines of gold kindled imaginations. It made the exploits of the seamen seem grander and more worthwhile. And it tempted others to seek their fortunes in the islands.

Mendaña received a lukewarm welcome from the governor. He had brought back nothing of value, only limping ships and sick seamen. Determined to make his voyage seem a success, Mendaña decided to try again in 1595. He gathered his wife, her three brothers, and three hundred hopeful colonists in four ships. After a long and quarrelsome journey, they landed in Santa Cruz hundreds of miles to the east of the central Solomons. Two months later, Mendaña died and the colonists struggled back to the Philippines.

There were efforts by other explorers, and sometimes it seemed every island found in the Pacific was called the Solomons. But maps were not exact and the true islands were too small. It was impossible for the Solomons to stay isolated forever. In the 1800s Europeans ranged the world founding and fighting over colonies.

In the Solomons a pattern had been set: initial distrust, then a period of hope, followed by misunderstandings, exploitation, and brutality. This chain of events, begun with Mendaña and his sailors, was to be repeated over and over again.

Chapter 5

INTRODUCTION TO
THE WORLD

By 1800 the Pacific Ocean was becoming known. Chinese tea was drunk in English parlors. Trading ships often went island-hopping to take on supplies and perhaps pick up something exotic that might have a market in Europe or America. Between 1798 and 1803, four ships recorded stops in the Solomons.

Englishmen and Americans captained the first ships through the islands. The traders' route would take them to Australia where they sold their cargos and then to China where they filled their holds with tea. They would pass through the Solomons on their way home, crossing to the north between Choiseul and the Shortland Islands. By 1830, ships were stopping several times a year to trade iron hoops for coconuts, fruits, wood, and the edible taro root. Some traders made a special stop at the Solomons to get tortoiseshell and pigs to exchange for sandalwood in New Hebrides (present-day Vanuatu). Both sides felt they were exchanging items of little worth for ones with high value. Each side, depending on its viewpoint, bargained successfully or was cheated. Occasionally there were disputes, sometimes ending in death.

A hand-colored woodcut shows the crew of a whaling ship with their quarry.

Beginning in the 1820s, whaling ships hunted near the islands. The ships traded for food, often stopping year after year at the same villages. Islanders, attracted by the ships, would leave the Solomons and sign on to be sailors. They brought home English words and valuables from the outside world: caps, calico, playing cards, and especially tobacco and guns. They also too often brought back death, in the form of smallpox, chicken pox, dysentery, measles, and mumps.

MISSIONARIES

A decade after the first whalers had tempted men from their villages, the missionaries arrived to save the islands for Christianity. The French Roman Catholic bishop Jean-Baptiste Epalle sailed into Astrolabe Harbor on Santa Isabel in 1845. The islanders were happy to trade and willing to listen. It seemed the

A Catholic church on Guadalcanal

mission would be a success. After several weeks, Bishop Epalle decided to take his ships farther up the bay. He was warned not to go. "If you are a friend of ours, you will be their enemy." Choosing not to listen, the bishop anchored his boat offshore. Sixty canoes escorted him onto the beach where he was met by a crowd of people. He was surrounded and attacked. He died three days later. The remaining missionaries moved to Makira Harbor, Makira, where they stayed for about a year. Then they moved to Tikopia, but seemed to have disappeared by 1851. The Catholics did not return to the Solomons for almost fifty years.

The next missionary effort was made in 1850 when the Australasian Board of Missions was formed. The Anglican bishop of New Zealand, George Augustus Selwyn, planned his strategy differently than the Catholic missionaries had. He invited young boys from the villages to return with him to New Zealand and

Norfolk Island for religious training. In 1857 alone, one ship stopped at sixty-six islands and brought back thirty-five students. Some of these boys returned several times and finally came back to the islands as missionaries.

BLACKBIRDERS AND RECRUITERS

The missionaries' efforts were complicated by a more menacing visitor, the *blackbirder.* Blackbirder was the name given to the ships and men who cruised the islands of the South Pacific in the late 1860s and 1870s, collecting men for the sugar and cotton plantations of Fiji and Queensland, Australia. The white European planters had been given land to develop into plantations, but they lacked the labor to work the land. In the 1860s, although some plantation workers were European, many more came from India as indentured servants. (An indentured servant promises to work for a certain period of time and for a certain set payment.) Recruiting the Indians was expensive. Many of them could not adapt to the harsh work on the plantations and died. The plantation owners turned to the Pacific Islands for a closer, less-expensive, and more-reliable source for workers. In August 1863 a retired sea captain and plantation owner named Robert Towns brought the first boatload of Solomon Islanders to Queensland. By the early 1870s recruiting ships were a common sight.

In the earliest years of the labor trade, ships were not particular about how they persuaded the islanders to volunteer. Frequently blackbirders disguised their ships as missionary ships flying a missionary flag. Young men were lured on board and then imprisoned in the hold. Ship captains held out promise of presents, bribed "big men" to paint pictures of adventure for the young recruits, or simply kidnapped them. Many accounts described sailors dropping harpoons or pig iron into the canoes, circling the ships, and then fishing the overturned men out of the water. Once on board, the islanders sometimes tried to escape by diving over the ship's rail or by attacking the captain and crew. A seaman tells of how his captain had bags of broken glass placed on deck to scatter in case the islanders did attack, either on the ship or from the shore. It became dangerous for ships to put into port for food and water.

Soon blackbirding became less possible, less profitable, and less necessary. By the middle of the 1870s there was a British government agent on each recruiting ship to guard against violence. Thousands of islanders had gone to plantations on Fiji, Queensland, Samoa, and New Caledonia for two years and returned. They had brought back boxes full of goods. Especially valued were Snyder rifles, tobacco, and axes. For a price, middlemen in the coastal towns helped to attract recruits. The record of one transaction lists gifts of "400 sticks of tobacco, 3 axes, 2 dozen fishhooks, lengths of fishing line, 4 knives, a belt sheath and knife, a pair of scissors, clay pipes, a dozen boxes of matches, and some cloth" for one recruit. But recruits often needed no persuading, and many actively volunteered. For some, going abroad meant escaping punishment for breaking a taboo or committing a crime. For most, work on a plantation satisfied the need for adventure and status. The recruits were exposed to Christianity, which some adopted. Boxes of goods were exchanged for the shell money needed to marry. The two years of plantation labor became an accepted passage into adulthood.

Chapter 6

COLONIALISM: DOMINATION AND MISUNDERSTANDING

BRITAIN TAKES CONTROL

Survival in the Solomon Islands has always been hard. Blood feuds, the ravages of disease, and in some areas, head-hunting contributed to a short life span. However, in the fifty years between 1850 and 1900, European diseases such as measles, smallpox, and dysentery swept in epidemics through villages. The Europeans, particularly the British, who brought these diseases began with the idea of doing good.

To protect trade, control violence, and in their own eyes, to help the Solomon Islanders, Britain put the Solomon Islands under loose control in 1877. A British high commissioner ruled from Fiji. His authority was mainly over British citizens, not other Europeans or Solomon Islanders. Nevertheless, the British sent out ships when they felt it was necessary to punish islands or individuals. Germany and France also had colonies in the South Seas. In a bit of housekeeping in 1886, the European leaders parceled out the islands among themselves. France took the

Society Islands, New Caledonia, and New Hebrides. Germany took Samoa and New Guinea. They also demanded some of the western islands, including Bougainville, Choiseul, and Santa Isabel. Britain claimed the southern and eastern Solomons. The islanders were not consulted.

Gradually Britain extended and consolidated its control. In 1893 Captain Hubert Gibson scrawled a declaration on a sheet of paper announcing that New Georgia, Makira, Guadalcanal, and Malaita were to fall within the British Protectorates. In 1896 Charles Morris Woodford became the first British resident commissioner to protect the rights of trade and British citizens in the islands. There were fifty Europeans living in the Solomons. Thirty-three of them were British.

The area of the protectorate continued to grow. By 1899, Woodford had added Rennell and the other far southern and eastern islands. Also in that year, Germany returned Choiseul, the Shortlands, and Ontong Java to Britain to end arguments over the ownership of Samoa.

Woodford had been a naturalist in the Solomons in the 1880s. He spoke a few words in the Solomon languages and had some understanding of the people. He chose to balance British aggression with diplomacy. In addition to organizing a militia of white traders, he rewarded friendly villagers with gifts and influence.

SELLING LAND FOR PLANTATIONS

England instructed Woodford to pay people to help administer the islands. But he was given only enough money to hire a few Fijian police and to build a home. To increase his income, he decided to sell land in the Solomons. As a first step, he sailed through the islands labeling apparently unowned land as "wasteland." But the islanders had different ideas about property. Property in the Solomons was owned by groups, not individuals. An individual simply used it. Furthermore, villages and crops were shifted every few years. Land could appear vacant when it really was only being rested.

Woodford operated by European laws. The Waste Land Regulation passed in 1900 allowed Woodford to sell any land he determined was not occupied. The islanders sold because of pressure or to pay debts, but islanders and Europeans had different understandings of the nature of the transactions taking place. Islanders often sold land with the belief that the land would revert back to them when the person who made the purchase died. Also, for the islanders, purchasing the land did not mean purchasing the trees on the land, nor would purchasing the trees mean that the land had been purchased. Disagreements arose between Solomon Islanders as to who owned the land, whose ancestors had originally cultivated it, and who had the right to sell it. Disputed cases were brought to court or land was sold secretly. Land rights remain one of the greatest problems in the Solomons today. In 1990 most of the cases were decided in favor of the purchaser.

One of the biggest purchasers was Captain William Hamilton. People who worked for his company dived for pearls in Santa Isabel and captured turtles to sell the tortoiseshell. Captain Hamilton paid more taxes than anyone else in the Solomons. He had no trouble buying a large number of islands in the Manning Strait between Choiseul and Santa Isabel. When his business declined, he sold land to Burns Philp, a company that became one

A coconut plantation

of the most powerful in the Solomons. In 1912 England amended the Waste Land Regulations so that Europeans could not buy land directly from Solomon Islanders. Burns Philp avoided the restriction by obtaining a 999-year lease from the resident commissioner to purchase lands it needed. Shortly after, Lever Brothers bought 80,000 acres (32,400 hectares) of land and obtained 999-year leases on more. It was the beginning of the Solomon Islands plantations.

PLANTATION WORKERS

About thirty thousand Solomon Islanders sailed to overseas plantations, especially in Queensland, between 1870 and 1911. One-third of them never came back, either dying or choosing to

These photos taken in the 1920s show Malaitan men who went to work on plantations. Here they are wearing decorations for feasting.

stay abroad. Others came home for a time and then returned once or twice more. Almost 70 percent of the plantation workers had come from the hills and mountains of Malaita. Now many of them chose to work in the new Solomon Islands plantations. By 1912 twenty other companies had joined Burns Philp and Lever Brothers. Plantations grew coconuts and produced *copra,* dried coconut meat, from which oil is pressed. Some also tried cacao, rice, tobacco, and oil palm.

Adjustment to plantation life was difficult. There was no one language that everyone could understand. Pijin English, which had developed in the first contacts between Europeans and islanders, became the common speech. People from one tribe, who had been taught all their lives to mistrust and fear members of other tribes, now had to work with them. Sometimes men became friends. Sometimes there was hostility.

Village people did not distinguish between master and servant, but the European plantation owners did. Overseers expected complete obedience. Plantation owners treated the islanders as if they were slaves. Some plantations, such as Lever Brothers, had a reputation for being run with a minimum of trouble. But on other plantations, workers were whipped and humiliated. In return the workers stole from the overseers and sometimes attacked them.

It was a complicated relationship. The islanders got trade goods and later cash. On the better-run plantations, there were adequate food and shelter and the work was reasonable. When many years later plantations no longer hired temporary laborers, they were missed. But the friction between the European owners, overseers, and workers contributed to an atmosphere of suspicion that continues to the present day.

CHRISTIANITY

Christianity was another powerful Western influence in the Solomons. The Church of England's Melanesian Mission had been the only missionary group since 1852, when the Roman Catholics left the islands. In 1900 the Anglican Church claimed twelve thousand members. Other churches now began sending missionaries into the Solomons. The Catholic mission returned. Then the Queensland Kanaka Mission started converting laborers on the plantations in Queensland. When these converts came back to Malaita, they formed the basis of the South Seas Evangelical Mission. In 1914 the Seventh-Day Adventists arrived and soon became influential.

Chapter 7

A NEW VIEW
OF THE WORLD

England had called it a "pacification campaign," and it had been a success. Peace of a kind had come to the Solomon Islands in 1929. Head-hunting had been almost eliminated from the bush. Most Solomon Islanders were Christians. The British lived in the capital of Tulagi on the Florida Islands and ran the government or stayed in district offices and collected taxes. The British and Australian coconut plantations of Lever Brothers, Burns Philp, and W.R. Carpenter were showing a profit. Forty-two thousand tons (about 38 thousand metric tons) of copra were exported in 1928. It was not high quality, because Solomon Islands copra was dried by smoke instead of the sun or hot air. This meant that oil from this copra could be used only in soap, not purer products like margarine. However, the Solomon Islands controlled 5 percent of the world market, and the owners were satisfied. Even individual islanders had begun collecting fallen coconuts and drying copra. In 1928 3,000 tons (2,721 metric tons) of the total copra production came from individual islanders.

THE DEPRESSION

The world depression hit the Solomons in 1930. Orders for all products fell sharply. In addition, a beetle attacked the coconut trees, causing the nuts to fall before they were ripe. Plantation owners tried to lay off their workers, but the two- and three-year contracts that had tied the workers to the plantations now kept the owners from letting them go. Plantations tried rubber, but it took too many specialized workers. They tried rice and the birds ate it. By 1934 all but the largest plantations were empty.

British traders also had problems. A few Chinese had come to the Solomons in 1920 to work at plantations as cooks or carpenters. One by one they had opened stores or restaurants or gone into trade with money from relatives in China. They were willing to go into the villages to trade instead of waiting for the Solomon Islanders to come to them. The Chinese restaurants were glad to serve the islanders, who were not allowed to eat at European restaurants. The Chinese supported and helped each other. In the pre-World War II capital of Tulagi, the Chinese stores and houses multiplied until they occupied a substantial section of the town. The British traders could not compete and most left.

The depression did not hurt the islanders as much as the five hundred Europeans, who had the best jobs, which were not open to the islanders. The islanders worked as carpenters, servants, and laborers on the plantations and in the timber business.

HEADMEN

Gradually the Solomon Islanders were drawn into the British administration. It became common for district officers to appoint headmen for each village. They were supposed to keep count of the people in the village for the purpose of taxation. They also were supposed to make sure that the villagers worked on community projects such as clearing government paths. In criminal cases, the leaders were middlemen between the village and British courts. Often these headmen were considered more important by the British than they were by their village, but it was a start toward self-rule.

ALEC WICKHAM

A few of the islanders who had worked on ships or plantations or volunteered for mission schools stayed abroad. One of the most famous is Alec Wickham, son of a British planter and a Solomon Islands woman. While studying dentistry in Australia, Wickham became a competitive swimmer. By 1920 he had set world records in the fifty-yard sprint and the high dive. Alec Wickham's sprint stroke was a variation of a stroke used for years in New Georgia Island in the Solomons. Today it is known as the Australian crawl, or freestyle.

WORLD WAR II

Even though there were still problems, the Solomon Islands were calm in the 1930s and were making small changes for the better. Then World War II struck. The actual invasion and combat only lasted two years, but its effects changed the Solomon Islanders and their relationship with Europeans forever.

In late 1941 the Japanese began systematically stepping down through the Pacific reaching for Australia. They knew if they could establish a base in the Pacific Islands, they could effectively block the convoy routes between the United States and Australia. In January 1942 the Japanese captured Rabaul, the administrative capital of New Guinea. By March they were in the Solomon Shortland Islands. In May the Japanese occupied Tulagi, the capital of the Solomons, located in the Florida Islands. They entered Guadalcanal and began construction of an airfield. European planters, traders, and plantation owners fled. The Chinese closed their shops and hid in the mountains. With the foreigners gone, the islanders were left to face the Japanese almost alone.

When the Japanese landed they had the same need as Mendaña's men did four hundred years before: food. Before the Europeans escaped, they burned and destroyed all they could to deprive the Japanese of support. All that was left were remnants of the plantations and the village gardens. At first the Japanese established their bases and left the islanders alone. In some areas, the islanders cooperated with the invaders. Later, as the war came closer, the Japanese used guns to get what they couldn't get by request. People were tortured, churches were looted, and villages and gardens were stripped.

Less than a hundred nonislanders remained in the Solomons. They organized themselves into "coast watchers." They set up makeshift radio stations in the hills to broadcast ship movements and positions. Islanders acted as scouts and spied for the coast watchers. Uasaia Sotuto set up an espionage network around the Buka Passage (north of Bougainville, in present-day Papua New Guinea). Bill Bennett, son of a New Zealand father and a Solomon Islands mother, was a chief scout for coast watcher D.C. Kennedy. Together Bennett and Kennedy not only "watched" the coast but

American forces land on Guadalcanal in August 1942.

sank a Japanese whaleboat, captured prisoners, and engaged in hand-to-hand combat.

At midnight on August 6, 1942, the Americans slid silently into the waters around Guadalcanal for their first major offensive against the Japanese in the Solomons. Before the Japanese were driven out in 1944, eighty thousand men in airplanes, battleships, submarines, and on foot had battled throughout the islands.

The islanders did not participate directly in the major engagements, but they conducted guerrilla strikes either in groups or singly. Tales of these warriors still are heard. There was Seni from the Western Province, who captured rifles one by one until he had enough to form his own fighting force. There was Nagatu, who, together with his men, gathered weapons from a detachment of sleeping Japanese and then surrounded and captured them. Perhaps the most famous was Jacob Vouza, who was caught when a Japanese company made a surprise landing on the Guadalcanal

Left: B-24 bombers fly over the Solomon Islands during World War II.
Right: A wrecked Japanese airplane is part of a war museum on Guadalcanal.

beach. When Japanese soldiers saw Vouza was carrying a small, souvenir American flag, they grabbed him, tied him to a tree, and demanded information about American positions. Angered when Vouza refused to talk, the soldiers bayoneted him twice and left him for dead. Vouza chewed through the rope and struggled back to the American camp. His information led to the capture of eight hundred Japanese.

To support the Allied forces, twenty-five hundred Solomon Islanders joined the Solomon Island Labour Corps. The islanders unloaded cargo, carried back the bodies of dead soldiers, and brought ammunition to the front lines. The islanders worked with both black and white American soldiers. The Americans treated the islanders with respect and generosity. For the first time, Solomon Islanders saw black people in positions of trust and responsibility.

IDEAS OF INDEPENDENCE

Finally the war was over. The Japanese were gone. Then the Americans left too. The debris of war remained. So many sunken

A photograph of some U.S. marines who fought in the Pacific in World War II (left). This memorial is dedicated to the men who died on Guadalcanal in World War II (right).

ships sat rusting in the sea channel separating Guadalcanal and the Florida Islands that it became known as Iron Bottom Sound. Almost every Christian village had a church bell made from empty shell casings.

The war left its greatest mark, however, in the minds of the Solomon Islanders. The respect and fear that they had had for the British and their acceptance of being second-class citizens in their own country had been shaken by their experience of war and their exposure to the Americans. The country became restless under British rule.

Malaita especially was influenced by the experiences of the young Malaitan men who had served in the Solomon Island Labour Corps. There was a history of rebellion in Malaita. For the most part, it was not Christian. There were no Europeans living in or near the villages. There had been a bloody revolt and then great retributions in 1927 when the British had tried to collect a head tax. Two of the returning Malaitan men, Nori and Aliki

Nono'oohimae, began to talk to the people about joining together. In union there would be strength to present their needs to the British governor. They asked, "Why should we pay taxes when we get nothing in return?" Their organization was called *Maasina Rule,* meaning "rule of brotherhood." The leaders decided the Malaitans would not work on plantations, they would refuse to pay taxes, they would not participate in census taking, and they would do no other work for the government for which they were not well paid.

The movement spread to the islands of Makira, Guadalcanal, Gela, and Isabel. Communal villages were built. Some farms were started to produce pineapples and coconuts, and communal gardens were planted. The British government could not believe that the Malaitans, with their history of feuding, were working together. But they knew that it would be dangerous for them if the Malaitans and the others succeeded in challenging their authority. Labor and cooperation were needed to rebuild the copra plantations. There were some efforts at negotiation, but they failed. With the collaboration of some of the headmen that the British had appointed, the government sent soldiers to apprehend the Maasina Rule leaders. Nine men were arrested and sentenced to six years hard labor. In the following months, hundreds of others also were imprisoned for failure to pay taxes. Gradually the movement weakened and then failed.

INDEPENDENCE

The changes that had started, however, were not to be stopped. Colonialism had lost its appeal in the world. Rather than yielding a profit, it was an expense. Countries ruling other countries far

Peter Kenilorea, the Solomons' first prime minister

from their shores were criticized in the world community. One step at a time, the Solomons became independent. In 1960 there was an Executive and Legislative Council with twenty-one members, including six islanders who advised but did not rule. By 1963 the Legislative Council was elected rather than appointed. By 1967 the Council had become a Legislative Assembly, headed by Solomon Mamaloni, with the power to make most laws and decisions. The British governor kept veto power only. The Solomons were officially declared independent in 1978, with Peter Kenilorea from south Malaita as the country's first prime minister. Mamaloni and Kenilorea have been the Solomons' most influential leaders in these first years of independence. In 1993 Bill Hilly was elected prime minister, with the help of an alliance of seven different groups opposed to Mamaloni. But Mamaloni was reelected prime minister in 1994. The Solomons retain their connection with Great Britain only as a member of the Commonwealth. Members of the Commonwealth, which includes large countries like Canada as well as small ones like the Solomon Islands, choose a governor-general to act as the representative of the British Queen. Through the governor-general, Britain advises and performs ceremonial duties.

Coils, made from red honeyeater feathers, were used for bride prices on the Santa Cruz Islands. Now they are treasured and passed down through generations.

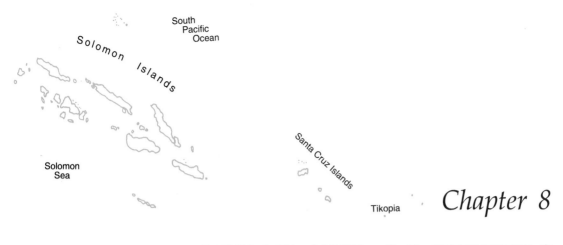

South
Pacific
Ocean

Solomon Islands

Solomon
Sea

Santa Cruz Islands

Tikopia

Chapter 8

SEPARATE SOCIETIES

The societies of the Solomon Islands were separated for so long by mountains, forests, and feuds, that each area developed its own distinct ways. Some of these ways survive only in folklore. Some are still practiced today.

CUSTOMS

On Santa Cruz Islands, feathers were once used as money. A female honeyeater bird was tied to a twig painted with a sticky substance called birdlime. When her mate responded to her calls for freedom, he became stuck to the birdlime. The islanders plucked the soft, red feathers from his neck and back and then let him go. Artisans wove the red honeyeater feathers along with brown dove feathers into coils two inches (five centimeters) wide and as long as thirty feet (nine meters) or more. Sometimes it took feathers from five hundred birds to make one coil. The coils were used as money in ceremonies and for bride prices. Although they are seldom made anymore, the remaining ones are treasured and passed down from one generation to the next.

To coastal people like those in Santa Ana and Santa Catalina, a canoe meant life or death. Because of this, there were many rituals surrounding canoes. When a war canoe was launched, a captive was sacrificed. Canoe houses were built and blessed. Skulls of ancestors decorating the houses were supposed to protect the canoes. Before their formal initiation into manhood, boys slept, fasted, and prayed inside the canoe houses. On Santa Ana and Santa Catalina, this seclusion could last as long as one or two years. Human sacrifice was stopped in the early 1900s, and hurricanes have destroyed most of the houses, but the memories and stories remain.

Depending on the island, sharks are considered a menace or a dinner. But on Savo Island, the shark is sacred. The Savo Islanders believe that sharks and humans are kin and that sharks have a human spirit. Nearby on the artificial island of Lualasi near Malaita, priests learn to call sharks, luring them to a channel between the islands. Pigs are thrown to the captive sharks as sacrifices. In earlier times, the sacrifices were human.

On the eastern islands, fishing is sometimes done with kites. A string and hook are tied to the kite as a kite tail. Then the men floating in the canoe allow the kite to sail out over the water. When a fish bites the hook, it and the kite are reeled in.

WHO ARE THE ISLANDERS?

Who are the Solomon Islanders? Did they come to the islands in separate migrations, or do they vary so much because different groups of people lived in isolation for generations? In some cases, it is obvious that they are genetically different peoples. The brown, straight-haired Polynesians on the outer islands are not the same as the darker, curly-haired Melanesians on Malaita.

Scientists suggest that the coasts of the islands might have been

*The jungle undergrowth and the destructive tropical climate
have erased almost all clues to early civilization in the Solomons.*

closer to the mainlands of Indonesia and Papua New Guinea
when sea levels were much lower because of the vast sheets of ice
deposited during the Ice Ages. There is general agreement that the
Solomons were probably populated by wanderers on rafts and in
canoes. Perhaps these were restless explorers, much like
Mendaña's men were, when they came upon the Solomons.
Perhaps they were driven by hunger, war, or simply became lost.
No one knows. The jungle has saved few clues. The tropical
climate does not preserve evidence of earlier cultures. Tropical
undergrowth covers anything that remains and the hot, moist
climate speeds its decay.

Yet, in Papua New Guinea charcoal that was burned at a
campfire twenty-seven thousand years ago has been found. Also
in Papua New Guinea, as well as in Fiji, New Caledonia, and the
Tonga Islands, archaeologists have unearthed three-thousand-year-
old pottery they call Lapita ware. Finally, in the small eastern
island of Tikopia, there is a hand-laid stone road winding around

No one can say for certain from where the ancestors of these children came.

a crater lake. It is 3 feet (0.9 meter) wide and 1.5 miles (2.4 kilometers) long. The people who built it about 900 B.C. have vanished, leaving no other trace of their existence.

DIVISION BY GROUPS

Some scientists divide the Solomon Islanders into groups according to the languages they speak. One of these is Austronesian, which is translated as "southern island." This family of languages is spoken in Indonesia and many of the islands of the South Pacific. The other group is Papuan and is most easily described as "languages that are not Austronesian."

On paper, the division seems neat and clear. But there are more than sixty languages on the Solomons, not including dialects. Neither skin color nor dwelling place seems to determine which language group a culture will use. Some claim that all the languages have one, ancient origin. If that is true, no one knows where that first language was spoken.

South
Pacific
Ocean

Solomon Islands

Malaita

Honiara

Solomon
Sea

Chapter 9

KWAIO: LIFE IN THE BUSH

The Kwaio are a bush people. Small Kwaio villages, often with
four or fewer families, lie scattered among the mountains of
Malaita, which may rise as high as 2,297 feet (700 meters) above
sea level. Often several settlements are built close together
separated by a strip of dense bush. The land is red clay,
mudstone, and limestone. Streams intersect forest paths. It rains
frequently. A hundred years ago each of the six large islands of
the Solomons had considerable bush populations. Now many of
the villages have moved closer to the coasts or have lost their
young people to the plantations and the towns.

There are one or two dwelling houses in the center of a
clearing. Higher up are houses where men sleep, especially young
adults, old men, and priests. Sometimes younger men build a
sleeping place separate from their fathers and uncles. All the
dwellings are rectangular, usually with only one room and very
little furniture. The buildings where cooking and eating take place
are smoky inside.

On the lower slopes of the hill are huts where women go
during their monthly menstruation and during childbirth. Because

A tourist visits with local women.

of strict taboos, women and their work are kept separate from men. Women's powers are believed to be dangerous to men and to endanger the community's relationship with their ancestors. The house, the village, the latrines, and the streams all have a male and a female place. Bamboo water pipes, the low door, women's sleeping mats, and the place outside under the eaves where the pigs rest after foraging all day are on the women's side.

Each house has its own gardens. Around the settlement, often near a shrine, medicinal and magical plants are grown. Some, like the many-colored crotons and coleus, are valued for their leaves. Some, like ginger, are valued for their scent, and some are prized for their curing powers.

The heart of the settlement is the ancestral shrine. This grove of trees, set a distance from the village, has never been cut and towers over the rest of the jungle. Inside the grove it is dark and quiet with spots of sunlight that have broken through the branches. Here priests are placed at death, pigs are sacrificed, and sacred ceremonies take place.

Even women enjoy a good pipe now and then.

CLOTHING

In their ancestors' times, the Kwaio wore little clothing. The men might have had a loincloth made of bark that had been stripped from the trees, dried, then soaked in water and hammered with a mallet to make it pliable. Children ran naked. Very young girls wore a bark belt that was changed to an apron and a belt of beads when they married.

Today men wear shorts and perhaps a T-shirt. Women wear a small cloth apron. Some wear T-shirts, skirts, or cloth dresses, especially when they come down to the markets in towns below the mountain.

SMOKING AND CHEWING

Throughout Melanesia many villagers smoke. Even children frequently carry clay or wooden pipes. Many people also chew betel, a mild stimulant that relieves fatigue and hunger. They carry the ingredients in a small bag that is hung around the neck: areca nuts, powdered lime, and the leaves or pods of the betel pepper. Chewing betel stains gums and lips bright red. The Kwaio also may have black teeth, not from betel but from a paste that needs to be applied frequently. They believe that this paste is both decorative and provides protection from tooth decay.

DIVISION OF LABOR

Each person in the village has work. Women care for their garden and their own and the family's pigs. Pigs are treated almost like pets and are not used as an everyday food. They are eaten at feasts and on other religious occasions. Women also must carry firewood, take the produce to weekly markets, do the cleaning, and raise the children. Daughters help their mothers as soon as they can walk, but sons are free from most responsibility. Boys hunt birds or opossums, practice spear throwing, and wrestle. Teenagers treat pig stealing as a game, although it is one that may have serious consequences if they are caught.

Men have their own individual gardens and perhaps another one planted for a special future feast. They build the houses, do some hunting, and supervise and protect their families. A machete, a large, heavy knife, is like a man's third hand. With it he slashes away the undergrowth that chokes the paths between the settlements, to the shrines, and to the market. If the soil wears out or the elders feel too many taboos have been broken, then the village goes through the complicated process of moving itself. This is a serious decision, and some Kwaio hamlets haven't moved for decades.

These boys on Rennell Island, showing off their pets,
probably will be plantation workers when they are older.

In August through November the cannarium almond is ripe.
Everyone in the Solomons goes nutting. Special hammers are
made for cracking the nuts. After groups pick nuts, the shells are
cracked open. The nuts are either dried in the sun or smoked
above the cooking fire and then stored. It is fun for everyone—a
little work and a lot of visiting.

As boys grow older they become restless and leave for jobs on
the plantations or in towns. Far from their villages, one man out
of four never marries. When they do marry, the man may be in
his thirties or forties and the bride still a teenager.

HONORING ANCESTORS

On important occasions people all over the world give feasts
involving celebration, religion, and ritual. Among the many feasts
the Kwaio hold, some of the more important are those given for
remembrance and enjoyment, but they are much more than just

A group of men on Malaita sing together and accompany themselves on traditonal wooden percussion instruments.

simple get-togethers. They involve the exchange of valuables, power, prestige, and the strengthening of family bonds. Kwaio who want to give a feast but have no reason will make an opportunity. When the decision is made, the family cultivates taro gardens and fattens pigs. *Bata*, the strings of shells the Kwaio use for money in traditional exchanges, is accumulated for ceremonial gifts and as payment for more pigs. The family prepares special coconut and taro puddings, selects and clears the feasting site, and hires panpipe musicians.

On the evening of the feast, related families stream toward the site carrying pigs and long strings of bata hanging from poles. As they gather and sit, the feast giver calls out names and presents the bata. The amount is remembered. Similar amounts are returned at the next feast. Speeches are made. Puddings, leaf-wrapped pork, and taro are distributed to each visiting family to roast around the fire. Panpipers play undulating melodies on tubes of bamboo tied together by twisted fibers. Small groups of men sing traditional songs. And the families talk, laugh, and eat until sunrise.

It is important to satisfy the ancestors because they have great influence over the living. If they are pleased, the tribe and the person will have *mana,* spiritual power. If a taboo is violated, a sacred word misspoken, or a pig not properly sacrificed, the ancestors may become angry. Sickness or death, crop failure, or natural disaster are all blamed on the displeasure of the ever-present spirits, who are strong and independent.

CONTINUING CHANGES

The life of the Kwaio and other bush people has changed drastically in the past hundred years and is continuing to change today. The Kwaio used to engage in warfare and blood feuds. That is no longer the case, but they are still a feared, strong, and independent people proud of their traditions and their ways of life. Many Kwaio are afraid that they will lose their customs. They fear that the histories of their ancestors will be forgotten and taboos ignored. Young Kwaio men still leave for jobs far from their mountains, and some have become Christian. A few Christian villages have been built in the lower hills. A hospital was constructed near the Kwaio in 1966 and shortly afterward an airfield was built. Logging companies negotiate to clear land of trees. In reaction, some Kwaio men have spent years writing down records of shrines, land ownership, and genealogies for future generations. The struggle to participate in the economy of the country and yet to preserve tradition is an increasingly difficult challenge for these bush people.

South
Pacific
Ocean

Solomon Islands

Malaita

Honiara

Guadalcanal

Solomon
Sea

Chapter 10

THE MAN-MADE ISLANDS

Down the slopes from the village clearings in the hills and mountains of Malaita are the most unusual settlements in the Solomons. These are the artificial islands dotting Malaita's lagoons. Built for access to the sea and safety from island warfare, they are the most crowded of the Solomons' villages.

Sulufou in the Lau Lagoon was one of the earliest built. It is 80 yards (73 meters) long and only 30 yards (27 meters) wide and lies in a lagoon 30 miles (48 kilometers) long and 2 miles (3.2 kilometers) across. There are fifty other islands in the lagoon. More islands are being added gradually.

HOMES, SHOPS, AND MEETING PLACES

The streets are laid out in arcs with the houses arranged so that two families live back to back. Each family faces a path. In some places the paths are so narrow that it is difficult to walk. Most houses have one room and are built of palm and thatch. The

*Artificial islands sit on a mass of stones that
have been rafted to the site.*

floors are sand, coral gravel, or raised wooden planks. As is
common elsewhere in the Solomons, the kitchen is built next to,
not in, the house.

Some islands have small shops that carry essentials such as
soap, a limited amount of food, matches, and personal items. For
the Christians, one of the larger central islands holds a church
and a social center. The islanders are drawn there not only for
religion but for politics, business, and entertainment as well.
Gatherings give a feeling of community to the islands.

Most islands, Christian or traditional, have a men's house
where unmarried men may sleep and gossip. The traditional
islands had the women's areas facing Malaita and the men's
facing the sea. In the past, when the Solomons were more warlike,
any invader would have to pass through the women's section to
attack and possibly would be weakened by violating religious
taboos.

Paddling canoes helps men to develop powerful bodies. This man is opening his catch of giant clams.

WAY OF LIFE

Gardens and firewood are on the mainland, and people make several trips every day. Lagoon men are known for their powerful bodies developed from paddling canoes back and forth. Close to the islands, men standing waist high in water fish with nets or lines. They catch turtles and sometimes sharks, in addition to smaller fish for food and for sale. Twice a week they bring their catch to the market. Some of it, like shark fins for making shark-fin soup, is exported to Asian countries.

In the seas of the artificial islands and around Gela and South Malaita, divers search for the shells used to make shell money. They either shape the money themselves or sell the raw shells to mainland villages. Before they built the artificial islands, these people used to live on the coast. They were called saltwater

A man with a tattoo on his face wears shell money.

people and were indistinguishable from other coastal peoples. Now their island culture and lifestyle set them apart from the other communities of the Solomons.

Overcrowding and lack of opportunity have caused many of the artificial-island dwellers to leave for jobs and homes on Auki or Honiara. They have built villages in the south of Malaita and in the capital of Honiara on Guadalcanal. Some of them have achieved important business and government posts. But there is a homesickness for the beauty and feeling of community on the artificial islands. Most of these people return, if only for vacation. They say life is easy there, no hills, close friends, and less work.

Most Solomon Islanders are Christians. Women join their church choir (above)
and families gather at the village church (below).

Chapter 11

A CHRISTIAN VILLAGE

Most people in the Solomon Islands live neither in the bush nor in the town. They make their homes in small Christian villages of one or two hundred people. These villages stretch along the coasts and rise up into the hills. Small groups of houses are separated by trees or perhaps a small coconut plantation owned by one of the families. Each group is linked to the others by a carefully kept path.

Certain things in the village are shared. In some villages there is a water tap for washing clothes and showering, though many use a stream nearby. Extended family groups share their drier for the copra. A copra drier is basically a large, open wooden box containing four or five bottomless oil drums laid horizontally end to end. A fire is built in the drums with the smoke escaping out one end. There is a wire mesh stretched over the top of the box and always a roof over the whole structure. The coconut halves lie on the mesh, where they dry in the heat.

Near the center of the village is a church, a sports field, and a passenger or guest house in which the minister, government officials, or health workers stay.

HOUSEHOLDS

Homes may be on the ground or raised on stilts with the family's canoes sheltered below. The typical house is roofed with

Palm thatch is woven onto a framework of light poles to construct a house.

sago palm leaves and walled with bamboo thatch woven onto a framework of light poles. Interior posts support the roof, and wooden walls divide the inside into separate rooms. There are few windows and little furniture, perhaps a chair or, more often, a section of tree trunk to sit on and sleeping mats or raised platforms for beds. The floor may be wooden planks, strips of dried betel nut tree trunk, or simply trodden earth or sand. Although every house has a fireplace, the kitchen is often in a separate building.

Each home has a garden for family food, but the gardeners also may sell some of their crop so they can buy rice, canned tuna, and clothing, or pay school fees. There may be a stand of bananas, coconuts, oranges, limes, pineapples, mangoes, papaws, or cacao. Most of the copra and cacao sold today is from small village holdings. In the 1950s a blight spread through the islands and destroyed most of the taro plants. Now taro is saved for ceremonial use and has been replaced in the gardens by one of the many types of sweet potatoes.

Land is usually owned by groups of families or clans. It is not unusual for one clan to own the land and for individuals who belong to other clans to live, garden, and own trees on that land. A family group also may own the rights to fish in a certain place or off a certain reef.

In addition to growing produce, a household might share a trade store; raise chicken, pigs, and ducks; or make local artifacts, like bowls or string bags. Many people fish. Some use a hook and line either with or without bait. Others fish by bow and arrow or spear fish at night under torchlight. Sometimes people pull their canoes into a semicircle and beat the water to frighten the fish into their nets. Tuna, porpoises, garfish, turtles, and dugong are highly valued.

BELIEFS

Although most coastal villages are Christian, under the surface traditional beliefs often live. A garden might be cleared around a rock that formerly was a shrine to a shark deity. A certain snake in a path may be an omen of bad luck sent by an ancestor. In times of trouble, along with prayers to the Christian God, ancestors are relied on for strength and protection. The aid of a charm or a spirit's message heard in sleep can bring success in love or recovery from an illness. And on Guadalcanal there is the Vele man, who is believed to appear from nowhere and fatally curse someone with a wave of his magic bag.

Luangiua (Ontong
Java)

Solomon Islands

South
Pacific
Ocean

Malaita

Honiara

Solomon
Sea

Duff
Islands

Bellona

Rennell

Anuta

Tikopia

Chapter 12

POLYNESIAN ATOLLS

The Polynesian outliers are islands that lie outside the area that is called Polynesia. The Solomon Islands are in the area called Melanesia, but some islands in the Solomons are inhabited by people who speak Polynesian languages. These are called Polynesian outliers. Rennell and Bellona are south of the central chain of the Solomons. Luangiua (Ontong Java) is far to the north and Skiaiana is northeast. Taumako (Duff Islands), Pileni (Reef Islands), Tikopia, and Anuta are far to the east.

POLYNESIAN SETTLEMENTS

The people on these outliers are not Melanesian, like the rest of the Solomon Islanders, but Polynesian. Their skin is lighter and usually their hair is straighter. Some scientists think the islands might have originally been settled by one or a small group of lost Polynesian canoeists from an island such as Fiji, southeast of the Solomons. Blown off track, not knowing how to return, they

Left: A Polynesian mother and child   Right: Rennell Island is one of the largest existing high coral islands.

landed and stayed. Folktales speak of a small black people called *Hiti* who were wiped out by the Polynesian invaders.

However they arrived, these adventurers brought their culture with them. On Rennell, elders describe stone idols transported twenty generations ago by two canoes from Uvea (Wallis Island northeast of Fiji). A Christian convert is supposed to have smashed the idols in 1938.

In Tikopia, in addition to an ancient stone road, there are stone walls and what looks like a wharf. The islanders call it *Te Karoa.* It is not known if these are natural accumulations of rock or man-made, only that they are very old. Tikopia is evenly divided between lush tropical foliage, mountains, and a crater lake.

Bellona is a lagoon contained by steep limestone cliffs. It is 12 square miles (31 square kilometers). Bellona's neighbor Rennell is pure coral and almost 400 square miles (1036 square kilometers). Ontong Java is even larger. However, many of the outliers are nothing more than beaches of fine, white sand with no freshwater to support human settlement.

Some available seafood includes turtles and huge coconut crabs.

Polynesian villages tend to be larger than the Melanesian ones, but the homes are similar. They are built on a framework of poles with walls of woven coconut leaves and a roof of palm thatch or corrugated iron. Unlike the custom in the rest of the Solomons, the kitchen fireplace is usually inside the house instead of in a separate hut. Though the smoke is released through a fire hole, some smoke is welcome because it keeps out mosquitoes.

FOOD, CLOTHING, AND CUSTOMS

On Ontong Java the islanders eat coconut and taro. (The taro blight did not reach to most of the outliers.) They also eat bats, birds, and sea turtles as well as fish. There are few pigs on any of the islands. With little space and no traditional religious need for them, they just are not raised.

Tilapia fish from East Africa were introduced to Rennell to

This young woman has tattoos on her face and upper body.

relieve a food shortage in 1957. Like many introduced species, they found no natural enemies and have multiplied into the thousands. There also are huge coconut crabs and crayfish on Rennell that live in comparative safety because many of the islanders are vegetarians. Chewing betel is not popular, but on Ontong Java and Sikaiana the islanders make a fermented coconut juice drink.

On Tikopia there is a movement to save the old customs. For example, leaves from trees no longer grown in Tikopia are brought back from the Russell Islands. They are used to teach young girls how to weave traditional sleeping mats. Seeds exchanged between islands become the special trees that supply bark for bark cloth. Polynesian bark cloth is called *tapa*. It is made of the inner bark of these trees soaked in sea water and beaten

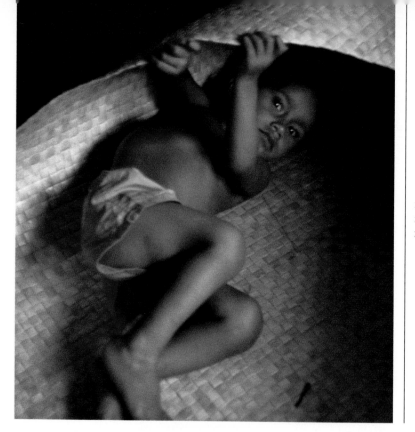

*Young boy preparing
to go to sleep, using
the hand-woven sleeping
mat as a blanket*

until paper thin. The finished tapa is dyed or stamped with bamboo stamps and displayed on special occasions. Sometimes tapa cloth may be worn. Then it is wound around the wearer's body and tucked in to fasten it. For everyday clothing, the women wear calico skirts and the men wear shorts.

Other old customs preserved by the Polynesians include tattooing the face and upper body with geometric designs. They also take pride in the ancient skill of building outrigger canoes. Outrigger canoes, seen in the Solomons since the first explorers, are dugouts with a float parallel to the main body of the canoe. The floats are attached to the canoes by long horizontal poles.

THE FUTURE

For a while there was the possibility that bauxite, the source for most of the world's aluminum, would be mined on Rennell. This

Outrigger canoes use a float parallel to the main body of the canoe.

would have been controversial, because some other Pacific islands have been almost destroyed by bauxite mining. But as yet, the cost of getting the ore outweighs the profit. The economy of the islands is based on coconut growing and fishing. The islanders also collect and sell trochus shells, and bêche-de-mer is considered a delicacy when dried and eaten.

The Polynesians were fortunate that the blackbirders who haunted Malaita and other islands in the Solomons did not consider it worth their while to travel to the outliers. But visits from the outside brought another form of extinction: disease. The British government was so concerned with the survival of the islanders in the 1930s that it forbade travel there without a special permit.

Now there is the opposite problem because population in many of the islands is growing too fast for the space. More and more Polynesians are migrating to Honiara.

Umbrellas provide shade for vendors at the Honiara market (above). A government building in Honiara (below)

Solomon Islands

South
Pacific
Ocean

Auki

Malaita

Honiara

Guadalcanal

Solomon
Sea

Chapter 13

TOWNS

A city brings to mind tall office buildings and traffic, crowded streets and apartment houses. Honiara, the capital of the Solomon Islands in Guadalcanal, is small for a city, with fewer than fifty thousand people. The Solomon Islanders refer to it as a town. Yet it has wide avenues and government buildings. Many of the other towns in the Solomons have only one main business street. In Auki, the largest town in Malaita, there is a gas station, a police district headquarters, a post office, Chinese trade stores, and a busy market. People come early in the morning with things to sell and hopes of things to buy. Small groups gather near the piers waiting for fishermen to return. Then the bargaining begins, with the fishermen slapping their catch out of the boat and the buyers smelling it for freshness. For some it is a regular ritual to come to the town, especially Honiara. People trade or just shop and visit and then return to their villages with special things found only in the town: clothes, bags of rice, kerosene, a good bush knife, a baseball hat, or a small radio.

Away from Guadalcanal and the larger islands, a town is often no more than a picture in a magazine or a half-remembered trip made years ago. For the people who live in these scatterings of

A Chinese-owned shop

houses on forgotten coasts or small settlements far up in the mountains, Honiara can be a two and a half day trip by a boat that visits each island just once a month. Only the Solomon Islands Broadcasting Corporation hurling out music and news links Honiara and the world to the rest of the Solomons.

LIFE IN HONIARA

To a villager in Honiara, for a first visit, the town is both strange and yet familiar. On the outskirts, houses made of thatch, timber, old wooden packing cases, or whatever is handy and inexpensive haphazardly dot the valley. Europeans like to construct their homes on the ridges looking down over the town. In Honiara itself, most people's houses are cement block with corrugated iron roofs. On some streets, Western-style homes display shiny cars parked in their driveways.

Honiara has a flourishing Chinatown of stores and restaurants and a Chinese population that has lived there since World War II. Wantoks make their own villages within the city bringing their food, language, and customs with them. But because village foods

A typical small-store complex in Honiara

like sweet potatoes are hard to find in town and expensive, they are supplemented with rice and locally canned tuna.

No matter how important a family is, they welcome relatives and visitors from their language group and support them as long as they care to stay. This has led to a large number of mostly unemployed young men, who drift through Honiara and strain its resources. It has been long accepted that males should leave their villages for a time and explore the outside world. In the past, this meant plantation labor. But now there is not enough work on the plantations for everyone, and Honiara is a more exciting place to be. Success in preventing disease and high birth rates have created a population where more than half the people are under twenty years old. In a village, welcoming a relative meant sharing a garden or, perhaps, building a thatch hut. Now with inflation making the cost of a pineapple more expensive in Honiara than in the United States, these young wanderers and other visitors create quite a burden on Honiara's population. Jully Sipolo, a Solomon Islands poet, describes the situation in her poem "Obligation":

My wages accounted for
Every cent spent, before payday
I've heaps of relatives to support
Out of obligation.

I have no priorities
My immediate family and wantoks
One hundred times removed
Are remembered,
Out of obligation.

Tobacco for an uncle who
Carried you as a tot.
Your poor mother who carried you
For nine months.
Be a good child and . . .
But I did not ask to be born.

One tenth to my God
One quarter to my spouse
The rest for my family
And payslip for me.

Obligation, not love,
Makes the world go round.
Dish out money while you are still rich
When you are broke, ask
Your wantok, knowing
You'll be given,
Out of obligation.

"Obligation" is from *Praying Parents,* copyright 1986, published by Aruligo Book Centre. Reprinted by permission of Jully Sipolo (Makini); Contact: Jules Makini, Gizo, Solomon Islands

An aerial view showing the bridge that leads travelers to Honiara.

The many stores, the avenues of flowering trees, and the opportunities for education and business bring an atmosphere to Honiara that draws in people from all over the Solomons. This is balanced by the problems of inflation, unemployment, and tensions between people from different backgrounds: coastal, island, and bush; European and islander. The politicians work to bring in more jobs. They speak of improving the villages so the young will not leave. There is talk of social reform and business connections to Australia, Japan, and other islands. Honiara and, to a lesser extent, the smaller towns hold many of the Solomons' hopes for the future.

Above: This garden had been cleared for planting by burning, a method that destroys minerals in the soil. Below: A woman weaves a basket (left) and another wears her dowry in her shell headpiece and money (right).

Chapter 14

THE ECONOMY: DREAMS AND REALITIES

The village economy in the Solomons always has been based on the seasonal round of planting and harvesting, producing food for family and relatives. Shell or feather money buys brides or pays for feasts. Carefully raised pigs are killed for a celebration and in an emergency. There are craftsmen in some villages who become famous for their specializations. One village may make woven baskets; another, feasting bowls. The coastal towns fish and the people in the bush grow fruits and sweet potatoes.

EXPORTS AND FOREIGN INVESTORS

In the old days barter, sometimes involving transactions between many villages, was more common than money. The outside world entered the Solomons in the 1800s when the English ships brought guns and iron to trade. The Solomon Islanders offered them trochus shells, bêche-de-mer, coconuts, and sometimes their young men for plantation labor. Englishmen settled in the Solomons, acting profitably as middlemen between the ships and the islanders. Other Europeans developed small coconut plantations. The plantations grew in size and were controlled by companies such as the English Pacific Island Company and Burns Philp. Later Lever Brothers, W.R. Carpenter, and the Fairymead Sugar Company joined them. The economics and the politics of the Solomons became dominated by foreign nations.

Today foreign companies still own many businesses and direct trade in the Solomons. But now the government negotiates contracts and purchases enough shares in the companies to exert some control. In 1977 thirty-two of the fifty-eight foreign-owned companies were Australian. Two of the biggest are Brewers Solomons Associates, Ltd., and Unilever, with numerous investments including cacao, coconuts, and timber. Japan, an enemy during World War II, is now a trading partner. Its Solomon Taiyo Limited, established in 1972, is the islands' major fishing operation. It employs more than eight hundred people and was the source of one-third of the Solomon Islands export earnings in 1985.

Japan is also the greatest importer of Solomon Islands products, especially timber. In some islands like Makira so many people have settled on the coast that there are vast stands of trees in presently uninhabited land. Many of the small villages once scattered throughout the mountains are deserted. The islanders' view is that the land and its timber still belong to the descendants of those who lived and worshiped on it, and parts of it are still sacred. Sometimes more than one group of people claim ownership. This causes conflict, especially when foreign nations

A logging operation on Vangunu Island

like Japan or Malaysia come in to cut lumber. Even in places like
Malaita, where the land is occupied, several groups may assert
their right to control timbered areas. It is one of the biggest
causes of court cases in the Solomons. Nevertheless, the
government estimates that at the rate forests are being cut down,
the available timber will not last long.

There also are worries that the huge nets of the commercial
fishing boats will empty the nearby seas of fish. It is a question of
quick profit versus long-term planning. Inflation is high and the
population is expanding. The Solomon Islands' most exportable
products are its natural resources. The temptation is to sell. But
what will happen to the people and the country if the forests and
the fish are gone?

At present, the Solomon Islands encourages the expansion of
the fishing industry, and more fish are being taken each year. In
1978 a 200-mile (322-kilometer) Exclusive Economic Zone was
declared so that only countries who had negotiated agreements
with the government could fish. This meant that the Solomons
had jurisdiction over more than 38,600 square miles (nearly

The first step in making copra involves chopping the coconut.

100,000 square kilometers) of the Pacific Ocean and the rich harvest of marine life, especially tuna, in it. In spite of this, there are continuing conflicts over which are Solomon Islands waters and which are international waters. In 1984 a large U.S.-owned fishing boat was detained for many months.

Another third of Solomon Islands exports comes from copra, coconuts, palm oils, and palm kernels. Coconut oil and palm oil traditionally have been used to make soap and as additions to prepared products such as cereal. Recent health reports suggest that these oils are not good for humans. Many companies are substituting other oils. This is certain to have an effect on Solomon Islands exports. Periodically, production falls because of

Normally roads are just passable, but when it rains they become much worse.

tremendous damage caused by cyclones such as the terrible Cyclone Namu in 1986. New land then must be found and new trees planted to make up for those destroyed.

Tobacco, rice, shells, and marine creatures such as crayfish and prawns also have been exported, but they are not yet a major part of the economy. Part of the problem in developing exports is transportation, overcoming the obstacles of mountain and ocean. Even getting a small load of vegetables to market is difficult. They first must be carried down steep slopes from the hill gardens to the dock. The small government boats or private transporters may stop only every other week. In the smallest anchorages they may pass by just once every month. Often the rocky shores and rough seas prevent a boat from docking. The vegetables must be loaded onto a small dinghy and maneuvered out to where a schooner is anchored. Then there is the long, damp voyage to Honiara or another central market. On Guadalcanal and other large islands where trucks make the trek, heavy rains frequently turn roads into pools of mud. Honiara and Gizo have international ports where vessels from Australia, New Zealand, England, Hong Kong,

A tourist shows a young man how to use binoculars.

Japan, and Singapore are regular visitors, but the major difficulty is in getting the products to those ports.

MINERALS

In 1968 an aerogeophysical survey was done. Planes flew over the islands taking special pictures that pinpointed mineral deposits. Copper, bauxite, phosphate, nickel, and cobalt deposits were found. People have panned gold from streams for years. Mining these minerals is a possible future option if a way can be found to do it economically.

TOURISM

The Solomon Islands would like to attract more tourists. The tourist bureau advertises clear, calm lagoon waters in which to swim, snorkel, scuba dive, or explore hundreds of small islands and coral reefs. There are war museums that hold the twisted iron remains from World War II battles and museums with war canoes and relics of an earlier age. In the evenings, the smaller resorts assure visitors of sunsets and peace, and the larger ones promise bamboo bands, dances, and feasts.

Snorkeling is a wonderful experience in the Solomons.
Inset: Hand-crafted souvenirs are available for tourists.

To help bring in tourists and to develop its economy generally, the Solomon Islands belongs to a number of organizations, including the Tourist Council of the South Pacific and the South Pacific Forum. Britain, Australia, and Japan give advice, lend money, and develop new projects each year. There are Peace Corps volunteers in the Solomons and volunteers from Canada, the United Kingdom, and the United Nations. Other aid comes from the World Bank, the International Monetary Fund, the European Union, and the South Pacific Bureau for Economic Cooperation.

THE ECONOMY

Economy in the Solomons means many different things. For the investor in the towns it means working with international companies, particularly Japanese and Australian ones, to bring in new industries and strengthen old ones. It involves fiscal plans, charts of economic growth, and trading schemes. For the workers living in Honiara, it means inflation, unions and strikes, and imported goods that are just a little too expensive to buy. For the villager, it is coconuts, carved bowls to sell, and maybe some cacao or a trade store. Prosperity is a new outboard motor for the canoe or a small stove in the house. In some small settlements in the bush the economy is still shell money, pigs, and barter. One out of seven households in 1979 had no cash income at all. The 85 percent of the people in the islands who live in the rural areas can meet most of their own needs. They only work for someone else when they need money for school fees, a bride price, a new boat, or extras such as clothes, rice, or canned tuna. Money is not the essential it is in more commercialized, modern societies.

Chapter 15

THE SOLOMONS TODAY

When Álvaro de Mendaña touched the shores of Santa Isabel in 1568, he forged a link between the Solomon Islands and the Western world. All over the globe, adventuresome and gold-hungry Europeans were exploring isolated lands. The countries and people whose lives they entered would never be the same.

CHANGES

The Solomons achieved independence in 1978, but remnants of colonialism stayed after independence. The British and the other European powers that made laws, sent missionaries, and traded in the Solomons in the 1800s and 1900s brought great change to the islands. This change has been both good and bad. The new religions brought peace to villages, but they changed centuries-old traditions. Western medicine doubled life expectancy, but it also doubled the population and doubled the need for food and shelter. Radios bring the outside world into the smallest settlements. The young people listen and become restless. They are tempted into the crowded areas of Honiara and provincial centers and depend for support on family and tribal ties. Timber sales and fishing fleets mean money and cars and imported goods. But they are destroying the ecology of the islands.

HEALTH ISSUES

In the past, the deadly rash of yaws, malarial fevers, hookworm, tuberculosis, and leprosy limited the life span of the average islander to only thirty years. The World Health Organization, a branch of the United Nations, worked with the islanders to eliminate these diseases. They sprayed a low concentration of DDT in the villages, distributed antibiotics, and educated local health workers. While the life span of the islanders has almost doubled, the war against disease is far from over. Because of ecological concerns, spraying is no longer carried out. Malaria, especially, is creeping back into the Solomons in new forms resistant to the old medicines. Crowding on the artificial islands makes their residents especially susceptible.

EDUCATION

The leaders of the Solomon Islands believe that education is one of the most important solutions for these problems. Before independence, children were gathered from widely separated villages and brought to boarding schools. Education was in English and had little to do with preparation for village life. Many families would keep one child in the village to learn about hunting, farming, food gathering, tribal history, and land ownership.

When it was time for high school, the tuition was more than one family group could pay. The extended family cooperated to finance the education of a small number of boys who boarded in Honiara for high school. Higher degrees meant scholarships and travel to Fiji, Papua New Guinea, or even Australia or England. In the late 1960s there were only three university graduates in the

King George High School complex near Honiara, Guadalcanal

whole population. By the 1970s sixty students were attending schools abroad. Each year after, the number has increased. Because it used to be so difficult to go to school or even find books in many villages, the literacy rate is less than 50 percent. This is gradually changing.

Kindergartens now are common in many places in the islands, and the first years of school are taught in Solomon Islands Pijin. The law states that all children must attend school for at least six years. There is a national system of three-year high schools in the larger rural districts. Health, agriculture, crafts, and local history are combined with the traditional academic curriculum. Students are being taught to appreciate their past.

CRAFTS

The Solomon Islanders used to be famous for constructing plank canoes. They cut wooden strips from trees and shaped them to the form of a boat. The planks were bound, or "sewn,"

A 1920 photograph shows Solomon Islanders in war canoes.

together with fibrous vines. Then the canoes were sealed with a crushed nut called a "putty nut." Some war canoes were 60 feet (18 meters) long and 5 feet (1.5 meters) wide. The bow and stern were decorated with intricate patterns or inlaid mother of pearl. Thirty to forty men paddled to the rhythm of a man sitting in the stern, who beat time on a drum. Smaller canoes were made for fishing, and even smaller ones were used when teaching the children how to paddle. War canoes are made no longer, and today's fishing canoes are usually dugouts or bought instead of sewn plank canoes. An outboard motor now substitutes for many hands. But fathers still fish and children still race, as much at home in the water as city children are hanging from the back of a pickup truck.

Another skill that is disappearing in the Solomons is the making of shell money. Shell money and barter or trade used to

After the bark of a tree trunk is removed, the trunk is shaped (left) and then hollowed out to make a dugout canoe (right).

be the only ways of exchanging goods in the Solomons. Now cash is taking the place of both. These days shell money is primarily involved in bride price and ceremonial exchanges. Although the Christian churches put limits on how much shell money can be demanded for a marriage, there are stories of payments of more than a thousand dollars worth of shells. The shells come from a small clamlike animal, *spondylus,* that grows near the bottom of the coral reefs. Tanakali, a village in Malaita, is famous for its shell making. The men dive to the bottom of the coral and collect the shells. Then they are broken into pieces just over 0.5 inch (12.5 millimeters) in diameter and ground into disks. The outer layers are rubbed off leaving the shells a dull red. The men drill holes with a hand drill and thread the shells on long, flexible sticks or on strings. It is the women's job to polish the money on sandstone until it is smooth and bright. The shell money circulates throughout the community in ceremony and exchange. It passes through the hands of one generation to the next.

A typical family meal

FOOD

Food is similar all over the central Solomons. Some people in town have an "English breakfast" of bread, navy biscuits, and tea or coffee with lots of sugar added. In the country, for both breakfast and dinner, the cook grates ripe coconuts that have fallen off a tree. She adds water and then squeezes this sweetened coconut juice into softened, boiled *kumara*, Pijin for "sweet potato." Early supper is the largest meal, perhaps with fish and baked or boiled kumara. Kumara is similar to the sweet potato known in the United States though not quite as sweet. Kumara can be white, purple, or red inside. It is favored because it has a three- to four-month growing period, compared to more than seven months for the traditional taro or a full year for the yam. It also does not have to be staked or very carefully tended.

A child is fed sweet coconut.

Coconut meat is seldom eaten alone except for that of very young coconuts, still hanging from the trees. Sometimes the juice is drunk and then the meat is eaten. After a coconut falls and begins to sprout, its center fills up with a sweet marshmallowy substance that is eaten as a snack.

Sometimes baked puddings are made with kumara, bananas, plantains, yams, or taro. The preparer arranges stones in concentric circles on the ground. Wood is piled on the stones, lit, and covered with another layer of stone. When the fire is out, vegetables are placed on a bed of leaves between the two layers of stone and baked from three hours to overnight.

In towns, because the different types of sweet potatoes are expensive, casseroles of rice, coconut water, and tuna fish are popular. Other foods include breadfruit, which has the texture of bread when it is baked, and cassava, a starchy root used to make tapioca in America and Europe. There also are tree ferns, nuts, wild fruits such as the Malay apple and the wild fig, bananas, sugarcane, corn, tomatoes, cucumbers, and snake beans that can grow up to 6 feet (1.8 meters) long.

LANGUAGE

Each culture has its own language, but Solomon Islands Pijin is the common language of the Solomons. Pijin began on the British ships that crisscrossed the Atlantic and Pacific Oceans to fish and trade. It grew from the broken pieces of sailors' English that were re-formed to fit the grammar and the language structure of each country it touched. The Pijins (or Pidgins) of the world are as complex, varied, and local in origin as any other local language. Solomon Islands Pijin spread from the ships to the plantations and to the towns, wherever islanders and foreigners mixed. Now it is the national language of the Solomons. Solomon Islands Pijin is enough like English to fool listeners into thinking that if they only try hard enough they will understand. For example, *Mami hem talen son blong hem fo stap long hom,* means "Mother told her son to stay home."

IDENTITY AND UNITY

An additional problem faced by the independent Solomons is to create a feeling of unity as one nation. Even now the islanders think of themselves as "Malaita men," "Polynesians," or "New Georgia people." As independence neared in 1977 there was a breakaway movement in the Western District. The people there felt that their blackness, the Christian Fellowship Church that they had developed, and their culture set them apart from the rest of the Solomons. Too much money, they said, was leaving their district and going to the government in Honiara. In 1983 the Fadanga group of Kwaio on Malaita declared East Kwaio a separate nation. They believed the elite in Honiara treated them no better than the colonial British had. With patience and compromise, both the Western District and East Kwaio won more local power and the movement faded. But tensions between the central government and the many separate groups still are there.

These tensions extend even to the far outlying atolls in the Pacific. From 1955 to 1977, people from the overpopulated Gilbert Islands were resettled in the Solomons. This brought yet another ethnic group into the islands. The new families made their homes and raised their children in the Solomons, but they were never accepted completely. At independence, the issue was whether they should have citizenship. It was finally agreed that a Gilbertese who had been born in the Solomons or who had married a resident could become a citizen.

PROGRESS AND THE FUTURE

There are problems in the Solomons as there are in all countries. There are stresses within the islands and pressures without. But the Solomons feel they are making progress. The government is more stable than in many developing countries. There are democratic elections. Prime ministers and representatives are replaced peacefully. Conflicts are settled by discussion and compromise. They call this process of give-and-take on both sides "the Pacific Way." The Solomon Islanders feel they are facing their problems and meeting them.

Man carving a club (left) and a young schoolgirl

Nowhere was pride in their country more fully shown than in the First South Pacific Mini Games in Honiara in 1981. Sixteen countries came to enjoy the hospitality of the Solomons. New Caledonia, French Polynesia, Papua New Guinea, Fiji, Western Samoa, American Samoa, the Cook Islands, Tonga, Wallis, Futuna, Vanuatu, Guam, Kitibatu, Nauru, Norfolk Island, and the North Marianas were all represented. People gave speeches and competed in events as part of the nation of the Solomon Islands. The Solomons now have a soccer team that competes internationally, with the goal of someday achieving a place in the World Cup playoffs.

Since that time, the Solomon Islands have increasingly taken an

A village on Malaita Island

international role not only in sports but economically and politically as well. The government is negotiating trade agreements with Japan. National sentiment supports rebel movements in neighboring Papua New Guinea. There is a Solomon Islands' representative at the United Nations, and in 1992 the Solomon Islands were the site for the South Pacific Forum, an alliance of surrounding Pacific countries including Australia and New Zealand. With the enormous distance between islands and the great variety of lifestyles and peoples, the Solomon Islands will always be balancing the strength of their individual parts with the need for national unity. It is difficult for a small nation to fairly participate in a complex world economy, but the Solomon Islands today are trying.

MAP KEY*

Alu	B1, B2	Mborokua, *island*	C3
Aola	D5	Mono Island	B1
Auki	C5	Mount Ghatere	B4
Avu Avu, *island*	D5	Mount Ire	C5
Barora Fa Island	B3	Mount Makarakomburu	D4
Barora Ite Island	B3	Mount Vangunu	C3
Bina	C5	Mount Vina Roni	C3
Blanche Channel	C3	Nanggala Hill	C3
Bougainville Strait	B2	New Georgia, *island*	C2, C3
Bradley Reefs	B5	New Georgia Group, *islands*	C2, C3
Buala	C4	New Georgia Sound	B2, B3, C3, C4
Buin	B2	Nggatokae Island	C3
Cape Alexander	B2	Nggela Pile, *island*	C4, C5
Cape Aracides	C5	Nggela Sule, *island*	C4
Cape Astrolabe	C5	Nukiki	B2
Cape Henslow	D5	Ontong Java, *island*	A4
Cape Recherche	D5	Oteotea	C5
Cape Zelee	D5	Papara	B2
Central, *province*	D4, D5	Pavuvu Island	C4
Central, *province*	C4, C5	Ranongga Island	C2
Choiseul, *island*	B2, B3	Rendova Island	C2, C3
Dai, *island*	B5	Rob Roy Island	B3
Dala	C5	Roncador Reef	A4
Fauabu	C5	Ronroni	C4
Fauro Island	B2	Russell Islands	C4
Florida Islands	C4, C5	San Cristobal, *island*	D5, D6
Ghizunabeana Islands	B3, B4	San Jorge Island	C4
Gizo Island	C2	Santa Ana I., *island*	D6
Gizo	C2	Santa Isabel, *island*	B3, B4, C4
Guadalcanal, *island*	C4, C5, D4, D5	Sasamungga	B2
Guadalcanal, *province*	C4, C5, D4, D5	Savo I., *island*	C4
Honiara	C4	Sealark Channel	C4, C5
Inakona	D4	Sepi	C4
Indispensable Strait	C4, C5	Shortland Islands	B1, B2
Iron Bottom Sound	C4, C5	Simbo Island	C2
Isabel, *province*	B3, B4, C3, C4	Star Harbour	D6
Kaoka Bay	D5	Stewart Islands	C6
Kirakira	D6	Susubona	C4
Kolombangara Island	B2, C2	Tangarare	D4
Kula Gulf	C2, C3	Tetepare Island	C3
Luti	B2	Thousand Ships Bay	C4
Makira, *province*	C6, D6	Three Sisters Islands	D6
Makira Harbour	D5	Tulaghi	C4
Malaita, *province*	A3, A4, A5, A6, B3, B4, B5, B6, C5, C6, D5	Uki Ni Masi Island	D5
Malaita, *island*	C5, D5	Ulawa Island	D6
Manning Strait	B3	Vaghena Island	B3
Maramasike, *island*	D5	Vangunu Island	C3
Maravari	B2	Vella Gulf	B2
Maravovo	C4	Vella Lavella, *island*	B2
Mbanika Island	C4	Visale	C4
Mbava Island	B2	Vonavona Island	C2
Mbola	D5	Western, *province*	B1, B2, B3, C1, C2, C3, C4
		Yandina	C4

*only includes the main group of the Solomon Islands

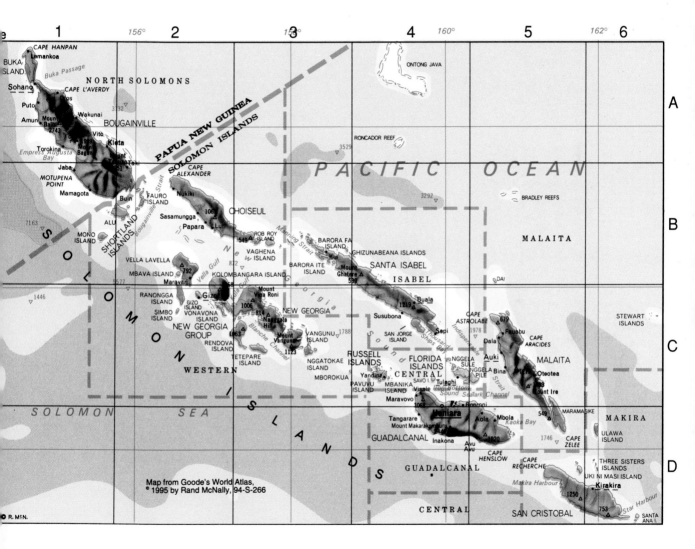

CAPE HANPAN
Lemankoa
BUKA
ISLAND
Buka Passage
Sohano
NORTH SOLOMONS
A
CAPE L'AVERDY
Puto
tos
Amun
Wakunai
Mount
Balbi
2743
BOUGAINVILLE
Vito
Torokina
Kieta
Bagun
Empress Augusta
Bay
Jaba
nt
3332
RONCADOR REEF
PAPUA NEW GUINEA
SOLOMON ISLANDS
3529
PACIFIC OCEAN
MOTUPENA
POINT
Mamagota
CAPE
ALEXANDER
Buin
Nukiki
B
FAURO
ISLAND
Buin
3292
BRADLEY REEFS
CHOISEUL
7163
Sasamungga
106
Luti
Papara
ALU
SHORTLAND
ISLANDS
548
ROB ROY
ISLAND
BARORA FA
Kia
GHIZUNABEANA ISLANDS
MALAITA
MONO
ISLAND
VAGHENA
ISLAND
BARORA
ITE
ISLAND
Mount
Ghatere
599
SANTA ISABEL
VELLA LAVELLA
792
822
ISABEL
DAI
MBAVA ISLAND
KOLOMBANGARA ISLAND
Maravari
5577
58
1446
RANONGGA
ISLAND
Mount
Veu Roni
Gizo
1006
1219
Buala
CAPE
ASTROLABE
679
Feuabu
STEWART
ISLANDS
SIMBO
ISLAND
GIZO
ISLAND
VONAVONA
ISLAND
814
Nagggala
Hill
NEW GEORGIA
Susubona
1978
Dala
CAPE
ARACIDES
C
NEW GEORGIA
GROUP
1063
Mount
Vangunu
VANGUNU
ISLAND
1788
Sepi
Auki
MALAITA
RENDOVA
ISLAND
1123
SAN JORGE
ISLAND
Bina
Oteotea
WESTERN
TETEPARE
ISLAND
NGGATOKAE
ISLAND
RUSSELL
ISLANDS
FLORIDA
ISLANDS
NGGELA
SULE
Mount Ire
MBOROKUA
CENTRAL
INGGELA
PILE
PAVUVU
ISLAND
SAVO I.
Tulaghi
SOLOMON
SEA
MBANIKA
ISLAND
Visale
Bonroni
549
MARAMASIKE
MAKIRA
Maravovo
Tangarare
Honiara
Aola
Mbola
Kaoka Bay
ULAWA
ISLAND
Mount Makarakomburu
Avu
Avu
1920
CAPE
ZELEE
1746
THREE SISTERS
ISLANDS
GUADALCANAL
Inakona
CAPE
HENSLOW
CAPE
RECHERCHE
UKI NI MASI ISLAND
Kirakira
D

Map from Goode's World Atlas,
© 1995 by Rand McNally, 94-S-266

GUADALCANAL
CENTRAL
SAN CRISTOBAL
1250
753
Star Harbour
SANTA
ANA I.

© R. McN.

MINI-FACTS AT A GLANCE

GENERAL INFORMATION

Official Name: Solomon Islands

Capital: Honiara

Government: The island nation of Solomon Islands is a parliamentary democracy and a member of the Commonwealth of Nations. A governor-general represents the British monarch and performs ceremonial duties. Honiara is the seat of Solomon Islands government and also home of the British High Commission and the governor-general. The legislative power rests with a National Parliament of 47 members. The prime minister, elected by Parliament, runs the government with help of a 15-member Cabinet. The judiciary includes a high court, a magistrate's court, and a system of small native courts throughout the islands.

For administrative purposes the country is divided into nine provinces and the capital territory of Honiara.

Religion: The constitution guarantees freedom of religion to all. The majority of the population follows Christianity (97 percent); other faiths practiced are Bahai and traditional beliefs. The chief Christian denominations are the Church of Melanesia (Anglican), Roman Catholic, and South Sea Evangelical Church.

Ethnic Composition: Melanesians are the largest ethnic group (94 percent of the population); followed by Polynesians, 4 percent; other Pacific Islanders, 1 percent; and Europeans, Asians, and others, 1 percent. The Melanesians are dark skinned and curly haired while the Polynesians are typically light, golden-brown skinned and straight haired.

Language: English is the official language but Solomon Islands Pijin (Pidgin), a combination of English and local languages, is the most widely used language. The two major language groups are the Austronesian and the Papuan. There are more than 60 languages spoken in the Solomons, not including dialects.

National Flag: A light blue and green field is divided diagonally by a narrow stripe from the lower left to the upper right corner. There are five white, five-pointed stars in the upper left.

National Emblem: The national emblem consists of an eagle and two frigate birds placed in the upper one-third of a central shield and weapons and two turtles in the lower two-thirds. An alligator and a shark are to the side of the shield, a canoe and a sun are above it, and a frigate bird and a scroll with the motto, "To lead is to serve," are placed below the shield.

National Anthem: "God Save Our Solomon Islands"

National Calendar: Gregorian

Money: Solomon Islands dollar (SI$) is the official currency. In March 1995 one SI$ was worth $0.30 in United States currency.

Membership in International Organizations: Asian Development Bank (ADB); Commonwealth of Nations; Economic and Social Commission for Asia and the Pacific (ESCAP); Group of 77 (G-77); International Monetary Fund (IMF); South Pacific Commission (SPC); South Pacific Forum (SPF); Melanesian Spearhead Group; United Nations (UN)

Weights and Measures: The metric system is in force.

Population: 386,000 (1993 estimates); 16 percent urban, 84 percent rural

Cities:

Honiara	35,300	(1990 estimate)
Gizo	3,700	
Auki	3,300	
Kirakira	2,600	
Buala	1,900	

(Population, except Honiara, based on 1986 estimates.)

GEOGRAPHY

Border: Extending in two parallel chains the Solomon Islands stretch about 900 mi. (1,448 km) over the South Pacific Ocean. The Solomon Islands are 3,000 mi.

(4,828 km) from the southern tip of China, 1,000 mi. (1,609 km) from Australia, and over 6,000 mi. (9,656 km) from North America.

Land: The island nation consists of some 993 islands; the largest islands are Guadalcanal, Choiseul, Malaita, New Georgia, Makira, and Santa Isabel. Choiseul, Santa Isabel, and Malaita follow one another on the South Pacific Ocean side. Makira, Guadalcanal, New Georgia, and Russell are on the Solomon Sea side. Bellona, Rennell, Sikaiana, Luangiua, Anuta, Fataka, Taumako, Tikopia, and Pileni are the Polynesian outlier islands separated by hundreds of miles of ocean from other Polynesian islands. Many of the outlier islands are nothing more than beaches of fine, white sand with little freshwater.

The islands differ greatly in their physiography, ranging from raised coral reefs to small atolls to mountain. The 300 mi. (483 km) long Pacific "Ring of Fire" snakes through the Solomon Islands; there are four active volcanoes. Earthquakes are more common than volcanic eruptions.

Highest Point: Mt. Makarakomburu, at 8,028 ft. (2,447 m) on Guadalcanal

Lowest Point: Sea level

Rivers: Rivers are short and fast-flowing with a potential for hydroelectricity. Lake Tegano on Rennell Island is the largest lake in the South Pacific.

Forests: On some islands trees cover as much as 90 percent of the area. Highlands have dense rain forests where some trees are 150 ft. (46 m) tall; the main trunk of a banyan tree can be 30 ft. (9 m) in circumference. Currently the rate of forest cutting is so high that the government estimates that the available timber will not last long. Islands are generally fringed with clumps of coconut palms and mangroves. Orchids are everywhere—some 230 varieties bloom in the Solomon Islands.

Wildlife: Solomon Islands' wildlife is varied. It includes various unique creatures like 8-inch (20 cm) long black spiders with yellow spots, 9-foot (2.7 m) pythons, Rana guppyi frogs that weigh 2.5 lbs. (1.1 kg), monitor lizards that can reach 5 ft. (1.5 m) in length, and the world's largest freshwater crocodiles. The wingspans of some butterflies are 8 to 11 in. (20 to 28 cm). Numerous varieties of birds include scarlet honeyeaters, parrots, hawks, eagles, storks, owls, herons, crested swifts, megapodes, and frigate birds. Twenty different species of mosquitoes thrive.

Climate: The tropical equatorial climate is hot and humid with a mean annual temperature of 80° F (26.6° C). It is rarely hotter than 80° F (26.6° C) or cooler than

70° F (21.1° C). Heavy rains are frequent but temperatures seldom vary. Annual rainfall varies from 60 to 200 in. (152 to 508 cm). Smaller islands suffer most from the seasonally violent weather; the eastern sections of the islands are the stormiest. The cyclone season lasts from December to April.

Greatest Distance: The Solomon Islands are spread over a 230,000 sq. mi. (595,700 sq km) area in the Pacific Ocean.

Area: 11,500 sq. mi. (29,785 sq km)

ECONOMY AND INDUSTRY

Agriculture: About 90 percent of the working population is involved in subsistence agriculture, but less than 2 percent of the land is under cultivation. Food is basically produced for family and relatives. The principal crops are coconuts, cocoa, sweet potatoes, taro, yams, vegetables, fruits, and oil palm. Some spices are cultivated for export. There are many different varieties of fruit trees: coconut, areca palm, cannarium almond, wild fig, banana, papaya, ivory nut, and malay apple are common. Land on atolls is too salty to grow crops. Pigs and cattle are raised, mostly for local use.

The surrounding seas are rich in fish. The chief fish caught are tuna, bonito, tunny, mackerel, porpoise, shellfish, sea cucumber, barracuda, shark, and garfish. Fish account for 30 percent of all export earnings.

Mining: There are small reserves of copper, gold, bauxite, lead, zinc, silver, asbestos, phosphate, nickel, and cobalt. Gold is the only mineral exported; people have been panning gold from streams for a long time. Lack of proper transportation is the biggest hurdle in the development of mineral resources.

Manufacturing: The economy is dominated by foreign nations, mainly Australia and Japan. The major manufacturing sectors are food processing, boatbuilding, coconut-based products, forestry, and the manufacturing of batteries, clothing, biscuits, tobacco, and soft drinks. Traditional handicrafts, including woodwork, shell inlay, mats, baskets, and shell jewelry, are becoming increasingly popular with tourists. Canning and freezing plants process fish for export. Energy is chiefly derived from hydroelectric and thermal power plants.

Transportation: There are no railroads on the Solomon Islands. In the early 1990s there were 1,300 mi. (2,100 km) of roads, of which some 10 percent were paved.

About one-half of the roads are privately owned by plantations. Heavy rains frequently turn the unpaved roads into pools of mud. Regular shipping services exist between the Solomon Islands and Australia, New Zealand, Papua New Guinea, Hong Kong, Japan, Singapore, and European ports. Interisland shipping operates between the islands. Honiara port is equipped to service oceangoing ships; Gizo, Yandina, and Noro are other major ports.

Solomon Airlines, the national airline, provides regular flights to Fiji, Nauru, Australia, and New Zealand. The international airport is Henderson Airfield, near Honiara. There are some 22 airstrips with scheduled flights.

Communication: The Solomon Islands Broadcasting Corporation provides daily radio service in Solomon Islands Pijin with some broadcasts in English. Several weekly and monthly publications are published both in English and Pijin. In the early 1990s there was one radio receiver per 9 persons and one telephone per 44 persons; there is no television service on the Solomon Islands.

Trade: The chief imports are machinery and transport equipment, manufactured goods, petroleum and lubricants, and food items. The major import sources are Australia, Japan, Singapore, New Zealand, and the United States. The chief export items are fish and fish products, wood and timber products, palm oil, palm kernels, cacao beans, and copra. The major export destinations are Japan, the United Kingdom, Australia, and Thailand.

EVERYDAY LIFE

Health: Health care is generally good, with hospitals and clinics available on almost all large islands. Western medicine has helped to increase life expectancy by controlling death by yaws, hookworm, and leprosy. Malaria and tuberculosis still are prevalent. Life expectancy stands at 69 years for males and 73 years for females. Infant mortality rate at 39 per 1,000 is moderately low. In the early 1990s there were about 9,900 persons per doctor and 190 people per hospital bed.

Education: Primary education is compulsory for six years, but it is not available free of charge. Schooling lasting for 11 years is divided into six years of primary, two years of middle, and three years of secondary education. The language of instruction is English. Kindergartens are now common in many villages and the first years of school are taught in Solomon Islands Pijin. Academic curriculum often is combined with health education, agriculture, crafts, and local history. Provincial

secondary schools provide vocational education, such as in different aspects of agriculture. Higher education is provided by the Solomon Islands College of Higher Education at Honiara, the Honiara Technical Institute, and the University of the South Pacific Solomon Islands Extension Center, also at Honiara. In the early 1990s the literacy rate was about 54 percent.

Holidays:
New Year's Day, January 1
Queen's Official Birthday, June 12
Independence Day, July 7
Christmas, December 25
Boxing Day, December 26
Movable holidays are Easter (April) and Whit Monday (May).

Culture: The Solomon Islands' National Museum and Cultural Center at Honiara promotes traditional culture including crafts, music, and dance. A good example of their craft is the plank canoes that were 60 ft. (18 m) long and 5 ft. (1.5 m) wide. Archaeological findings at the small eastern island of Tikopia includes a hand-laid stone road winding around a crater lake; this road was built about 900 B.C. Honiara has the National Library, a museum, a botanical garden, a hospital, and several churches and banks.

Society: The Solomon Islands society is very tightly knit. Supporting relatives is considered very important by all islanders. In some small villages a water tap is shared for washing clothes and showering; in others, a stream is used. The social structure varies from one island group to another. On Santa Cruz Islands money was made from feathers of honeyeater birds. Some Polynesians get their upper bodies and faces tattooed with geometric designs.

The Kwaio are a bush people living in the mountains of Malaita Island. They follow strict taboos. Women and their work are kept separate from men. An ancestral shrine is the heart of the settlement where sacred ceremonies take place. Many villagers smoke clay or wooden pipes. Many also chew betel leaves with areca nuts and powdered lime; betel chewing is supposed to relieve fatigue and hunger. Women share in caring for the gardens and the family pigs; they also carry firewood, take the produce to weekly markets, do the cleaning, and raise the children. Boys hunt birds or opossums and practice spear throwing and wrestling; girls tend to help their mothers as soon as they can walk.

Dress: Men generally wear shorts and a T-shirt. Some women wear T-shirts, skirts, and a small cloth apron.

Housing: Houses in towns are made of fiberboard or cement blocks with corrugated tin roofs. Low-cost housing projects have been built by the government at Honiara. Rural houses are made of wood and bamboo and are thatched with leaves; these are raised on stilts near the coastal areas.

The artificial islands dotting Malaita's lagoons have the most unusual settlements; these are the most crowded of the Solomon's villages. Houses are arranged in arcs so two families live back to back. Most houses are one room and built of palm and thatch; the floors are sand, coral, gravel, or raised wooden planks. The kitchen is built next to, not in, the house. In Christian villages the houses tend to be a little larger with separate rooms, a fireplace, and a few windows.

Food: The Solomon Islands diet is chiefly starchy vegetables like yams, sweet potatoes, taro, cassava, and bananas. Kumara and coconut milk and cream are very much part of the daily diet. In cities the sweet potatoes of the countryside are expensive, so people eat rice and tuna fish and drink soft drinks. Baked puddings are made with kumara, plantains, yams, or taro.

People on islands without freshwater cook with sea water and collect rainwater for drinking. Turtles and pigs are cooked and eaten at festivals. The Polynesians eat taro, coconuts, bats, birds, sea turtles, and fish. A fermented coconut juice drink is popular in the Polynesian islands.

Tourism: Tourism is centered on cruise ships. The islands offer tourists clear lagoons for swimming, snorkeling, scuba diving, or exploring coral reefs. To underwater divers they offer World War II planes and shipwrecks for exploring. The Solomon Islands belong to the Tourist Council of the South Pacific and the Melanesian Tourist Federation to promote further growth in tourism.

Sports and Recreation: Panpipe musicians play at feasts and festivals; they play melodies on tubes of bamboo tied together by twisted fibers. The Solomon Islands soccer team competes internationally.

Social Welfare: The National Provident Fund covers certain categories of wage earners. Most welfare is provided by church missions. Extended families take care of most of their disabled and needy relatives.

IMPORTANT DATES

1567—Álvaro de Mendaña leaves Callao, Peru, on an expedition to search for the Solomon Islands

1568—Mendaña reaches Ontong Java

1595—Mendaña decides to make another voyage to the Solomon Islands

1788—Two French ships, the *Boussale* and the *Astrolabe,* are shipwrecked on Vanikoro's Reef

1798-1803—Four trading ships stop at the Solomons

1826—The wreckage of two French ships is found for the first time

1831—The islands are given the name *Melanesia,* "Black Islands," by the French explorer Dumont d'Urville

1845—French missionary Jean-Baptist Epalle comes to the Solomon Islands

1850—The Australasian Board of Missions is formed; efforts are made to invite Solomon Islanders to New Zealand for religious training in Christianity

1850-1900—European diseases like measles, smallpox, and dysentery sweep through the islands in epidemic proportions

1852—The Roman Catholics leave the islands; the Church of England's Melanesian Mission starts missionary work

1863—The first boatload of Solomon Islanders arrives in Queensland, Australia, to work on plantations

1870-1911—Some 30,000 Solomon Islanders sail overseas to work in plantations

1877—The Solomon Islands are put loosely under British control

1886—The Solomon Islands are distributed by European powers among themselves; the Anglo-German Treaty establishes a German Protectorate over the northern Solomons

1893—Britain declares New Georgia, Makira, Guadalcanal, and Malaita under British protection

1896—Britain appoints the first British resident commissioner to protect the rights of trade and the British citizens in the Solomon Islands

1899—Britain adds southern and eastern islands to their Solomon Islands protectorates; Germany gives some of the islands back to Britain

1900—The Waste Land Regulation passes, it gives Britain the right to sell any land that is not occupied

1905—Large-scale plantations are started by British commercial interest

1912—Britain amends the Waste Land Regulation so that Europeans cannot buy land directly from the Islanders

1914—Seventh-Day Adventists arrive

1920—Some Chinese workers come to work on plantations

1927—The British attempt to collect a head tax from Malaitans; a bloody revolt and great retribution result

1928—A record 42,000 tons (38,000,000 kilograms) of coconut copra is exported

1930—The world economic depression hits the Solomon Islands

1934—As the depression forces small plantations to close, only the largest plantations are left operating

1942—During World War II the Japanese capture Rabaul, the administrative capital of New Guinea, and enter the Solomon Islands to establish a base in the Pacific

1944—The Japanese finally are driven out of the Solomon Islands

1944-1950—Maasina Rule spreads from Malaita throughout the central and eastern Solomons

1957—The tilapia fish from East Africa is introduced to Rennell Island in order to relieve a food shortage

1960—An Executive and Legislative Council is established with 21 members, including six appointed islanders who can advise but not rule

1963—The Legislative Council members are elected, not appointed

1967—The Legislative Council becomes the Legislative Assembly

1968—An aerogeophysical survey is done for pinpointing mineral deposits

1970—A new constitution provides the government with some local representation; eleven thousand cattle are shipped to the Solomon Islands

1971—A volcano near Santa Cruz erupts

1972—Japan establishes the Solomon Taiyo Limited company to handle the islands major fishing operation

1975—The protectorate is renamed as the Solomon Islands and granted self-government

1976—The National Provident Fund is established to provide social security benefits to all persons in paid employment

1977—The University of the Pacific opens a center in Honiara

1978—The Solomon Islands becomes an independent member of the Commonwealth of Nations; the Legislative Assembly becomes the National Parliament; a 200-mi. (322-km) exclusive economic zone is declared for restricted fishing by foreign countries

1980—The country holds its first elections

1981—The First South Pacific Mini Games are held in Honiara

1986—The Solomon Islands first large shopping complex, the NPF Plaza, is opened; heavy destruction is caused by Cyclone Namu; a fishing agreement is reached with the United States

1988—The Solomon Islands, Vanuatu, and Papua New Guinea form the Melanesian Spearhead Group (MSG) with a common aim of preserving Melanesian culture

1989—Solomon Mamaloni resigns as prime minister; the Solomon Islands ratifies the South-Pacific Nuclear-Free Zone Treaty

1991—Japan agrees to cease its drift-net fishing operations by the next year

1992—The Solomon Islands are the site for the South Pacific Forum; the government issues a stamp in honor of Álvaro de Mendaña; relations are strained with Papua New Guinea over the Bougainville civil war crisis

1993—Legislative elections are held; a project to establish several rural training centers is undertaken with the European Community's aid; Bill Hilly is elected prime minister

1994—Solomon Mamaloni is reelected prime minister

IMPORTANT PEOPLE

Ezekiel Alebua (1947-   ), political and government leader; prime minister in 1986

Dumont d'Urville (1790-1842), French explorer; named Solomon Islands *Melanesia,* the "Black Islands"

Jean-Baptist Epalle (?-1845), French Roman Catholic bishop; came to Santa Isabel Island

Bill Hilly, prime minister 1993-1994

Peter Kenilorea (1943-   ), political and government leader; leader of the United Party; Solomon Islands' first prime minister; head of the coalition government in 1984

Solomon Mamaloni (1943-   ), political and government leader; leader of the People's Alliance Party; head of Legislative Assembly in 1967; prime minister in 1981; was leader of opposition in the early 1990s; became prime minster again in late 1994

Álvaro de Mendaña (1541-95), Spanish explorer; nephew of Peru's Spanish governor Lope García de Castro; explored the Solomon Islands in search of gold

George Augustus Selwyn (1809-78), Anglican bishop of New Zealand; planned the strategy of inviting Solomon Islanders to visit New Zealand for religious training

Jully Sipolo (1953-   ), poet

Jacob Vouza, Solomon Islander who helped Americans capture eight hundred Japanese in World War II

Alec Wickham, son of a British planter and a Solomon Islands woman; competitive swimmer; set world records in the fifty-yard sprint and the high dive

Compiled by Chandrika Kaul

INDEX

Page numbers that appear in boldface type indicate illustrations

About the Author

Judith Diamond is a writer and an educational consultant for the Adult Learning Resource Center in Illinois. She has worked with, studied, and been friends with peoples from Southeast Asian cultures for over fifteen years. Roger Keesing, William Davenport, and David Akin, anthropologists; the Solomon Islands Embassy in New York; and the library staff at the Field Museum in Chicago, Illinois, have all been helpful in the preparation of this book.